Penguin Books

When to *Really* Worry

Dr Michael Carr-Gregg is one of Australia's highest profile psychologists and an internationally recognised authority on teenage behaviour. He was the founder of the world's first national support group for teenage cancer patients, CanTeen, and has been Executive Director of the New Zealand Drug Foundation, Associate Professor at the University of Melbourne's Department of Paediatrics and a political lobbyist. He is currently a consultant psychologist to many schools and national organisations, including Reach Out and beyondblue. He has been a regular on Melbourne radio 3AW, the resident parenting expert on Channel 7's *Sunrise* since 2005 and a regular on its *Morning Show*. He has written several bestselling books on parenting, including *Surviving Adolescents*, *The Princess Bitchface Syndrome* and *Real Wired Child*, and is the 'Agony Uncle' for *Girlfriend* magazine. He has won many awards for his work.

When to *Really* Worry

Mental health problems in teenagers and what to do about them

MICHAEL CARR-GREGG
ILLUSTRATIONS BY RON TANDBERG

Penguin Books

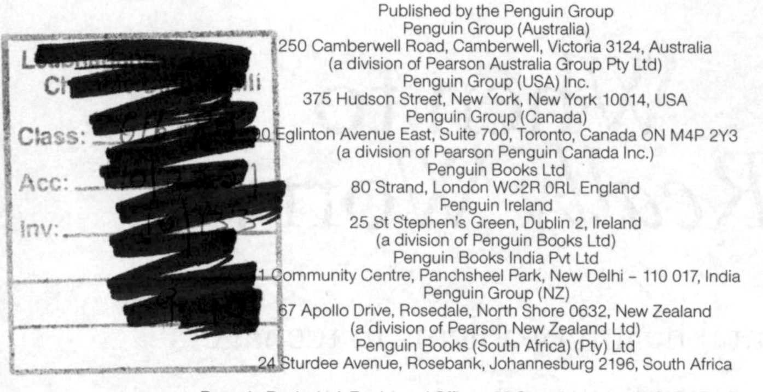

PENGUIN BOOKS

Published by the Penguin Group
Penguin Group (Australia)
250 Camberwell Road, Camberwell, Victoria 3124, Australia
(a division of Pearson Australia Group Pty Ltd)
Penguin Group (USA) Inc.
375 Hudson Street, New York, New York 10014, USA
Penguin Group (Canada)
90 Eglinton Avenue East, Suite 700, Toronto, Canada ON M4P 2Y3
(a division of Pearson Penguin Canada Inc.)
Penguin Books Ltd
80 Strand, London WC2R 0RL England
Penguin Ireland
25 St Stephen's Green, Dublin 2, Ireland
(a division of Penguin Books Ltd)
Penguin Books India Pvt Ltd
11 Community Centre, Panchsheel Park, New Delhi – 110 017, India
Penguin Group (NZ)
67 Apollo Drive, Rosedale, North Shore 0632, New Zealand
(a division of Pearson New Zealand Ltd)
Penguin Books (South Africa) (Pty) Ltd
24 Sturdee Avenue, Rosebank, Johannesburg 2196, South Africa

Penguin Books Ltd, Registered Offices: 80 Strand, London, WC2R 0RL, England

First published by Penguin Group (Australia), 2010

10 9 8 7 6 5 4 3 2 1

Design by Karen Trump © Penguin Group (Australia)
Illustrations by Ron Tandberg
Cover image © Photolibrary
Typeset in Simoncini Garamond by Post Pre-press Group, Brisbane, Queensland
Printed and bound in Australia by McPherson's Printing Group, Maryborough, Victoria

National Library of Australia
Cataloguing-in-Publication data:

Carr-Gregg, Michael.
When to really worry / Michael Carr-Gregg.
9780143009061 (pbk)
Includes index.
Bibliography.
Teenagers – Mental health.
Adolescent psychology.

616.8900835

penguin.com.au

In memory of Hannah and Lucy

Contents

Foreword

Raising happy, healthy children is one of the most difficult tasks a person can undertake. The path from childhood through adolescence to adulthood is a long and difficult one. It is peppered with risks to wellbeing, from the more commonplace problems associated with growing up, such as milder depression and anxiety, to the rarer and more frightening problems like psychosis. To add to these are the ever-increasing threats of bullying, drugs and inappropriate internet content.

From its first pages *When to Really Worry* is packed full of information, current statistics and invaluable resources. Not only does this book highlight the mental health risks faced by young people and their families, but it also points the reader to the most appropriate sources of further help. The journey from noticing that a problem exists to having it assessed and treated properly is often a lengthy and confusing one. The beauty of this book is that it provides enough information to determine whether or not parents should worry, and where they can go for appropriate help if need be.

Whether you are a parent, a teacher, a sports coach or even a health professional, this book is a must. For the uninitiated, the descriptions of the mental health problems are clear and concise. The case examples also provide a great insight into the problems as they are experienced by young people and their families. *When to Really Worry* is a terrific resource for anyone involved in the lives of young people.

Dr Simon Kinsella
B.Sc. (Hons), Dip. S.O. Hyp., PhD, MAPS
Honorary Fellow, Department of Psychiatry,
University of Melbourne

I'VE MISSED YOU DESPERATELY MUM!

Preface

This book was conceived after two events: the tragic death of Hannah Modra in early 2008, which I describe later in the book, and the declaration of a 'state of emergency' in youth mental health in a summit in October that same year.

We now know that 75 per cent of people who experience psychological problems first became ill before the age of 24. We also know that if we can diagnose and treat young people early, we can save them years, or in some cases a lifetime, of unhappiness. This reduces the likelihood of them self-medicating with alcohol or other drugs, along with the myriad academic, relationship and legal problems that plague the mentally ill. Yet despite all the hard work done by health promotion experts over the last few decades, recognition of mental health problems is still unacceptably low. It is estimated that less than 30 per cent of young people seek help for depression, anxiety and other psychological disorders.

This may in part be due to some parents having an 'ostrich

mentality', where they notice something strange about their son or daughter's behaviour, but out of ignorance or fear decide to ignore it in the hope that it will 'go away' or dismiss it as 'just a phase' typical of an adolescent. The longer this behaviour is ignored, the more hard-wired and complex the underlying problem may become and the harder it is to treat. This, of course, is compounded by the fact that unlike physical ailments, mental illnesses have fewer visible physical symptoms, and due to a combination of stigma, ignorance and prejudice it is so much harder for people to accept them as genuine illnesses.

Yet the good news, often overlooked in discussions of adolescent mental health, is that the vast majority of young people (estimates vary between 60 and 70 per cent) manage to get through their teenage years without any major problems. They may slam doors, sulk for hours, occasionally tell their parents to go forth and get multiplied, but much of this is pretty much par for the course for a teenager.

However, when it comes to teenagers, knowing the difference between warning signs and normal behaviour is not always easy. Yet as parents and carers of young people we are ultimately responsible for their health and wellbeing. Adolescents, despite their foot-stamping claims to the contrary, are not able to assess their own mental state and seek treatment. The distinguished Melbourne psychologist John Cheetham once said, 'There is no such thing as a perfect parent', but even so, all parents can learn to be better at parenting. This book aims to increase the emotional literacy of parents and in plain English explains what they can do when their teenagers lose their psychological moorings.

Michael Carr-Gregg
Melbourne, 2010

YOU'RE SUFFERING FROM A BAD CASE OF ADOLESCENCE
IS IT CURABLE?
IT'LL TAKE TIME
TANDBERG

Introduction

We like to think of young Australians as physically fit, bright, a little cynical and irreverent. But a 2007 Australian Institute of Health and Welfare report paints a somewhat contrary picture. While healthier than previous generations and certainly in better shape than their adult counterparts, when it comes to mental health our teens are in trouble. Mental health disorders are now the leading cause of disability among young Australians aged 15 to 24 and account for almost 50 per cent of the burden of disease in this age group.

Figures for children in early adolescence are also worrying. While most of our children are reasonably happy and healthy, a recent study by the Australian Childhood Foundation found that children aged 10 to 14 are experiencing some serious mental health problems. The report revealed that more than a third of children were anxious about terrorism or worried about having to fight in a war, and one in four believed the world would end before they reached adulthood. More than half were worried about being teased and bullied and one in ten were concerned about being called names because of their culture or nationality. Just under half of the children felt that they would never do well enough and a large number worried about the way they looked.

It is difficult to know whether mental health problems in children, adolescents and young people are increasing in frequency and severity or we are simply noticing them more. But the bottom line is that your teenager has a one in four chance of either suffering a mental illness or being close friends with someone who is. Australian Bureau of Statistics data from 2008 shows that 26 per cent of people aged 15 to 24 — about 650 000 people — suffered mental illnesses that year. These included many of the conditions that we will discuss in this book: depression, anxiety disorders (panic attacks, obsessive compulsive disorder, post-traumatic stress) and eating disorders. Around 13 per cent of them suffered conditions (e.g. psychosis) related to dependency on alcohol or other drugs (cannabis, sleeping pills, amphetamines and heroin). In many cases these illnesses, particularly depression, have the capacity to distort teenagers' moods, destroy their ability to think rationally and ultimately erode their desire to live. Untreated, these illnesses will persist into adulthood.

The reasons why some young people develop mental illnesses are many and varied. There are risk factors in the individual's genetic makeup, their family dynamics, their peer relationships, their schools and in the wider community. To go through each is beyond the scope of this book, but three areas warrant special mention.

A key community risk factor is the early sexualisation of young people, especially young women. An acclaimed 2007 report by the American Psychological Association found evidence that the proliferation of sexualised images of girls and young women in advertising, merchandising and the media was harmful to girls' self-image and healthy development. The report claimed that the sexualisation of girls and young women through toys (e.g. Bratz dolls, Bling Bling Barbie aka 'prosta-tots') and in magazines, TV shows, video games and music videos all had a negative effect, leading to a lack of confidence in their bodies as well as depression and eating disorders.

Another important risk factor is the paucity of good parenting. In 2008, former Australian of the Year Professor Fiona Stanley reported that one in five Australian parents were poor caregivers because they lacked the knowledge, skills and strategies to parent effectively and/or did not devote enough time to their kids because of excessive job commitments.

It seems that even some parents agree with Professor Stanley. An Australian Childhood Foundation report showed that 60 per cent of parents believed they could be better parents and 75 per cent believed parenting did not come naturally. It also found that 71 per cent of parents had difficulty finding time to enjoy activities with their children. The study revealed that more than half the parents surveyed lacked confidence in their parenting and 80 per cent wanted more information about parenting but were too afraid to ask for advice for fear of being stigmatised as a poor parent. Parents believed that toddlers (aged up to three) and teenagers (11 to 18) were the most challenging.

When it comes to individual risk factors, we need look no further than the fact that young people seem to be hitting puberty earlier than ever before. Bristol University's Institute of Child Health tracked the development of 14 000 children from birth and reported that one in six girls in Britain reached puberty by the age of eight. Many psychologists worry that the acceleration of growing up may be interfering with the latency period, a sort of 'waiting room' developmental phase when girls should be turning their backs on boys and bonding with their same-sex peers. Experience suggests that time in this 'waiting room' is crucial for the development of self-esteem and resilience, where children can experience a sense of belonging to their family, peers and school, learn vital social and emotional skills such as anger management, conflict resolution, problem solving and the capacity to name and recognise their own and other's thoughts and feelings. In this way they marshal their psychological resources in anticipation of puberty.

Early puberty is also exacerbated by the now-mainstream practice of hothouse parenting, where parents push their offspring to 'grow up' through accelerated learning programs, a punishing regimen of extracurricular activities and exposure to films and games that are way beyond their emotional, let alone cognitive, abilities – all in the mistaken belief that this will protect them from the slings and arrows of life. Sadly, in their attempts to do the very best for their children, these parents inadvertently make young people more fragile. As Hara Estroff Marano says, 'Hothouse parents raise teacup children – brittle and breakable, instead of strong and resilient.'

A combination of early puberty, sloppy parenting, peer pressure on steroids, the digital communication age and unprecedented mass media pressure all combine to short-circuit the latency period, preventing children from enjoying a free-range childhood where they develop a strong sense of self and an understanding of how they fit into the world. When a girl's body develops early, she is more likely to hook up with a boy and leave her group of girlfriends before the developmental work of the latency period is done. In the absence of sound parenting, ritual, tradition or spirituality, little wonder Australia is seeing so much mental illness in its young.

At present in Australia, the time that elapses between the

onset of the most common psychological problems in young people and their diagnosis and treatment is usually somewhere between five and fifteen years. This represents an enormous amount of human suffering that is largely preventable. This book aims to give parents the knowledge and strategies to recognise the most common signs and symptoms of mental problems and help their teenager get the right treatment.

In the first two chapters of the book I explain typical adolescent behaviour, and how you will know when to really worry. Chapter 3 explores depression, perhaps the best known of all mental illnesses, not least because it may lead to suicide. What is less widely understood is that depression may also occur when other mental illnesses such as anxiety disorders and eating disorders are left untreated.

In seeking treatment for mental illness, in most cases a GP will be your first port of call, and in Chapter 4 I discuss how to open a dialogue with your teenager to get them there, and how to find an adolescent-friendly GP. I also offer you some tips on navigating the sometimes frustrating process of assessment and treatment.

Chapter 5 discusses the most common treatments for mental illnesses so that you'll know what to expect. And in the remaining chapters I'll take you through the major mental illnesses, the specific signs and symptoms to look for and the prognosis for treatment and recovery.

Your role as a parent or caregiver is crucial. I can only give you the tools – you must be prepared to use them. As Dr Phil McGraw says, 'Life rewards action.' As adults, if we noticed a lump somewhere on our body we wouldn't let it fester away for a few days, a few weeks or over a year. Why then would we do the same with exceptionally odd behaviour or suicidal talk in a teenager? This book is an attempt to educate and inform parents so that they understand the symptoms and warning signs and feel confident in having an action plan – printing fact sheets, finding the best GP and being prepared to attend with their teenager, if necessary, whatever group training or therapy is recommended by the mental health specialist.

Obtaining support for yourself is equally important. All too often a combination of shame and guilt can stop parents from talking about their children's problems with other family members, friends or even other parents. Yet without strong support few people can deal with what is often described as the 'psychological disembowelment' of having a mentally ill teenager. If you are expecting your son or daughter to accept help, make sure you are willing to accept help, too.

TSUNAMI OF EMOTIONS . . .

Chapter 1

What to expect from teenagers

Someone once said that adolescence is living proof that Mother Nature has a sense of humour. As parents, we get to experience everything that we did to our parents when we were young. What goes around comes around! Yet many parents exhibit a retrograde amnesia for what it was like to be young, and can 'forget' the huge number of changes to which teenagers are subjected. In addition to the fact that teenagers' bodies go nuts, they also have to cope with a range of tectonic emotional, intellectual and social transitions.

Adolescence is a time of rapid change, challenge, exuberance, moodiness and health risks, culminating in the emergence of a young adult. Indeed, the word adolescence comes from the Latin word *adolescere*, which means 'to grow to maturity'. The physical changes are relatively easy to see, but if the emotional changes were visible they would be even more dramatic than the physical ones.

The mercurial emotions that are often evident in normal teens are characterised by 'feeling intensification', that is, the teenager tends to feel more intensely. It's amazing how many parents don't understand that the part of the teenage brain that 'feels' is not yet properly wired to the part that controls or calms down or 'puts the brakes on' behaviour, so that teenagers often feel as if they are being overwhelmed by a tsunami of emotions.

Not surprisingly, teenagers are also not very adept at reading the emotional cues of each other or adult carers, and can occasionally misinterpret relatively innocent remarks or requests, believing that someone is annoyed, distressed or overly critical when in fact they are just stating something.

Stages of adolescence

Psychologists divide adolescence into three stages: early, middle and late.

Early adolescence

Early adolescence is a time of immense physical changes with accompanying anxiety about appearance, body shape, growth and sexuality. The most common question asked at this age is 'Am I normal?' Early adolescents are understandably self-conscious and often overly sensitive about themselves, putting huge amounts of energy into worrying about personal qualities or defects that loom large in their imagination but are hardly recognisable to others.

The quiet, compliant child of recent memory is bombarded by a voice from within that tells them to turn away from childhood and childish things and to ignore their parents. The breaking of emotional bonds with parents is aided by changes in the brain that enable the early adolescents to see their parents through adult eyes. It is as if a neurological veil has lifted and the reaction is very often 'Oh my God! Who *are* these people?' This can often result in a withdrawal from the family, an intense desire to keep their lives private, and the monosyllabic communication ('good', 'yeah' and 'nah') that is so typical of their conversation.

Recent MRI research has found that the wild behaviour once blamed solely on 'raging hormones' should now be regarded as the by-product of two factors: an excess of hormones, *plus* a paucity of the cognitive controls needed for mature behaviour. A teenager's brain is not just an adult brain with fewer kilometres on the clock, but rather a high-powered one with steering problems *and* faulty brakes! A good idea for all parents is to imagine a tattoo on the forehead of their teenager that says 'Closed for Reconstruction'.

MRI studies show conclusively that young people's brains are growing and changing continually, and that in adolescence the brain is only about 80 per cent complete. The largest part, the cerebral cortex, is divided into lobes that mature from back to front. The last section to connect is the frontal lobe (just behind the forehead), which is responsible for cognitive processes such as reasoning, impulse control, prioritising, planning, and making astute judgments. Normally this mental merger is not completed until age 21–23 for girls and age 28–29 for boys.

A teenage brain's plasticity also means teenagers are more

vulnerable to external stressors. Teen brains, for example, are more susceptible than their adult counterparts to alcohol and other drugs. Binge drinking (more than five standard drinks for males, four for females) has been found to result in a smaller hippocampus – the part of the brain involved in information processing. Similarly, even though there is evidence that sleep is crucial for learning and memory, sadly teenagers are the most sleep-deprived segment of the population

Middle adolescence

This stage is dominated by a fierce interest in peers and a loosening/severing of emotional ties with the Neanderthal dorks that pass for 'parents'. Indeed, middle adolescents spurn adult control and support and use music, body piercing, hairstyles, tattoos and risk-taking behaviour to establish their own identity and individuality. Unsurprisingly, middle adolescence is replete with opportunities for communication breakdown, and relationships with parents can become torrid.

While risk-taking is seen as essential for psychological growth, unhealthy forms involve behaviour that may damage brain development or result in serious injury or death. This is far more likely to occur if a young person is bored, alienated and has little structure in their life.

Late adolescence

In late adolescence many young people have come to terms with their identity and are well on the way to defining and understanding their role in life. Relationships with adult carers are based much more on respect and affection as they realise that their parents aren't that bad after all, and perhaps also that they need their parents' food, car, washing machine, accommodation and discretionary income!

This stage is also about planning for the future, and research shows that the most successful are those who have an adult in their life to assist them with the process of setting goals and developing strategies. The presence of a charismatic adult makes all the difference.

A testing time

In making the transition from childhood to young adulthood adolescents need to:

- form a positive identity
- establish a set of good friends
- break the emotional bonds that bound them to their adult caregivers
- set meaningful vocational goals.

Of course, every teenager is unique. If you're lucky, yours will coast happily through all of these stages, but others will experience difficulties during just one stage, or through all of them. To complicate matters, those who appear to be happy may just be very good actors. The more parents understand the stages of adolescence the better prepared they will be to notice when things are wrong.

Keys to resilience

Of course, the best strategy is to try to prevent problems *before* they occur. Psychologists have found several important factors that determine a young person's physical and emotional wellbeing.

1. Having a mentor

Young people need an adult they can talk to, whom they draw strength from and who makes them feel safe, valued and listened to. It doesn't have to be a parent: it can be a friend, an uncle, a teacher, a coach or a grandparent – just as long as there is someone they feel connected to in the adult world, and who provides a positive role model.

2. Being good at something

Young people need to have regular activities that they enjoy and do well (sport, art, music, dance). This is important for their self-image and resilience as it gives them a sense of competence, teaches them about time management, allows them to mix with like-minded peers and exposes them to good adult role models.

3. Being emotionally intelligent

This is where parents come in. You need to model good communication (especially listening), to recognise and talk about emotions as being a normal part of life and to 'own' feelings and not blame others for them.

4. Feeling that life has meaning

Many studies show that young people who feel connected to something that transcends the material world are less likely to resort to smoking, drinking and using illicit drugs. This spirituality does not necessarily need to involve organised religion, but can simply be a deep respect for the sacredness of life on earth, or a sense of the connectedness of all things.

5. Thinking positively

'Self-talk' is the name psychologists give to the thousands of thoughts that run through our heads every day. There is a massive amount of evidence that positive self-talk promotes self-esteem and confidence. Teenagers who encourage themselves and tell themselves that they are doing okay are much more resilient and can cope more effectively with life stresses. Conversely, adolescents who tell themselves that they are failures will tend to have many more problems.

A GIRL THIRTEEN SHOULDN'T BE GOING OUT WITH A BOY EIGHTEEN
BUT HE HAS THE INTELLIGENCE OF A TEN YEAR OLD

Chapter 2
Is my teenager at risk?

As we saw in Chapter 1, there is no doubt that almost all teenagers would plead guilty to having the occasional mood swing, down day or angry outburst, but this should be regarded as normal. Typical media stereotypes of wild and unpredictable teenage behaviour (as seen in TV sitcoms and movies) are usually grossly inaccurate, and the vast majority of teenagers (around three-quarters) get through their adolescence unscathed.

But how do you know if they are really doing okay? Firstly, trust your instincts. You've lived with your teenager for more than a dozen years and you are in a unique position to notice any major and sustained changes in their behaviour. Secondly, remember that as the adult, you are responsible for their health and wellbeing – at least while they're under your roof. It is important to keep lines of communication open by learning to talk in an adolescent-friendly way.

Parents must be aware that along the road to young adulthood there are social toxins which threaten to derail even the most resilient young person. Living in a secular, disconnected society, the global economic downturn, terrorism, record levels of bullying and cyber harassment, family breakdown, peer pressure to dress provocatively, perform academically and become sexually active, alongside exposure to a veritable smorgasbord of alcoholic and narcotic seductions, mean that there will be many voices in the ears of our children and it is our job to ensure that ours is the loudest.

Yet despite parents being uniquely placed to notice mental and emotional problems in their teenagers, these are still notoriously difficult to diagnose for three main reasons. First, adolescence is a time of such change and tumult that it can be hard to work out what is usual and what is not. Secondly, teenagers are terrified of being seen as different, and therefore tend not to want to talk about what's worrying them. Third, many lack the experience/maturity to understand what's going on inside their heads let alone how to explain it to someone else.

After twenty-five years of working with young people, I have to say that a sure sign of when to worry is if your son or daughter has friends who are significantly older than themselves. In my experience, a 13-year-old hanging out with an 18-year-old almost invariably spells trouble with a capital T. For example, the natural habitat of an 18-year-old is often a pub, bar or nightclub – hardly appropriate for a 13-year-old.

Bumps in the road to adulthood

Psychologists have long argued that in order to complete the journey to young adulthood, teenagers need to accomplish four key tasks: form an identity, become independent, make strong friendships and find a place in the world. If the young person has no friends, seeks only to be in the company of their family or has no social pastimes, these may hint that all is not well.

Trouble with one task may not necessarily be cause for concern. However if a young person is struggling with two or more, a series of international studies suggests that this ratchets up the probability of a problem requiring professional assessment.

1. Forming an identity

The first task or 'job' for teenagers is to form a positive identity – answering the question 'Who am I?' But figuring out who you are is no picnic (plenty of adults still can't answer this one) and often involves teenagers asking huge life questions and attempting to make complex moral decisions. In essence it involves arriving at a point of self-understanding and self-acceptance.

One of the most effective ways that young people get to know who they are is through healthy risk-taking, where the risks involve testing their own competence through activities like sport, art, music, dance and drama. This not only alleviates boredom, gives their lives structure and allows them to socialise with peers with similar values, but also gives them the chance to meet other adults who share their passion and may become mentors.

2. Becoming independent

The second task is to achieve emotional autonomy and become independent of parents or adult carers in order to continue the process of becoming young adults themselves. This will inevitably mean making attachments outside the family.

3. Making strong friendships

Research suggests that at no other time in our lives is the desire to be with friends as strong as it is in adolescence. Young people place an incredibly high value on being accepted by their friends. Parents need to be sensitive to the importance of peer relationships, and to the fact that any disruption to, or break-up of, a friendship can be potentially devastating to a young person. There are few crimes worse than a parent pouring scorn on a young person's friendship group.

4. Finding a place in the world

In order to find a place in the world and achieve economic independence through a career direction or vocation, young people need to connect to school. Research suggests that one of the most important factors in academic success at school is forming a good relationship with teachers. While some people claim that they always knew their career direction, it is not unusual for young people to be very unsure about what they want to do when they leave school. If they are lucky they may meet a special person, visit a special place, or read a stirring book that will inspire them. Others are fortunate enough to complete an exchange term in another country, or even a year of travel, which can very often provide much-needed direction.

The father of positive psychology, Professor Martin Seligman, argues that all of us have core inner strengths and that one of the secrets to a happy life is to discover what these strengths are and to craft our lives so that every day we get to utilise them.

Risk factors in your teenager's worlds

Another useful way to think about your teenager's progress is to picture them as living in five separate, but often overlapping 'worlds': their inner world, their peer group, their family, their school, and the internet (or outside) world. Psychologists now know that each of these worlds contains both risk and protective factors that predict the extent of any emotional and behavioural problems. Listed below are signs that there are too many risk factors and not enough protective factors in each of your teenager's worlds.

Inner world

- Pervasive and unrelenting sadness
- Fierce and uncharacteristic irritability
- Inability to bounce back after stress
- Strange or unusual thoughts
- Rigid and inflexible thinking
- Sudden personality change
- Obsession with death/suicide
- Substance abuse

Peer group

- Withdrawal from normal social events
- Refusal to participate in clubs, hobbies, sports
- Sudden change in peer group

- Absence of friends
- Secrecy around peer group
- Displaying aggression and violence in peer group
- Having friends who self-harm
- Having friends who use illicit substances

Family

- Overly dependent on one or both parents
- Intense hatred of one or both parents
- Refusal to negotiate rules or boundaries
- Frequent conflict with siblings and other family members

School

- Sudden decline in academic performance
- Inattention or distractibility
- Refusal to do, or lying about, homework
- No relationship with teachers
- Hatred of school
- Truanting

Internet

- Being bullied or harassed online
- Internet addiction
- Only recreational activity is online
- Lying about amount of time spent online
- Intense irritability when asked to get offline
- Sexting
- Possessing and transmitting violent or degrading sexual images

Other worrying signs

Parents, schoolteachers and friends are frequently the first to recognise that an adolescent may be having noteworthy problems with emotions or behaviour. In addition to the risk factors discussed above, other signs may include:

- remains tearful, sullen and out of sorts for two weeks or more
- appears to lose interest in life and no longer enjoy things that used to give them pleasure

- has trouble sleeping
- is apathetic and excessively tired
- has trouble thinking and concentrating
- has extreme obsessions with appearance or food
- gains or loses a lot of weight
- repeats seemingly pointless behaviours
- has unexplained headaches, stomach aches and other pains
- shows persistently fierce and uncharacteristic irritability
- engages in uncharacteristic delinquent, thrill seeking or promiscuous behaviour
- makes comments like 'I feel rotten inside', 'I just want it all to end', or 'Soon I won't be a problem for everyone'.

If this aberrant behaviour occurs frequently, it suggests that the young person may be 'stuck', almost like a needle on a record, and someone needs to intervene. The last one is especially worrisome, as it may be hinting at suicidal thoughts (see Chapter 13).

Is their risk-taking healthy?

As we have seen, adolescence is a time of great change where young people take on new roles and responsibilities; renegotiate relationships with adults, peers, and the community; and experiment with things symbolic of adult life. Often these transitions depend on risk-taking behaviours, where adolescents test their skills and abilities against the wider world. Healthy risk-taking is a positive tool in an adolescent's life for discovering, developing, and consolidating his or her identity.

Unhealthy risk-taking, on the other hand, is often symptomatic of mental illness. For example, depression has been linked to a range of health risk behaviours such as smoking, alcohol use, illicit drug use, anorexia and overeating/morbid obesity. Other unhealthy risk-taking behaviour includes unprotected sex, thrill seeking, and delinquent behaviour (property damage, violence, petty crime).

Research suggests that adolescents who engage in one type of risk-taking behaviour are highly likely to engage in others. They are also likely to have one significant thing in common – a lack of connectedness to an adult caregiver. As noted in Chapter 1, feeling close to an adult role model (parent, family member, teacher, coach etc) is fundamental to positive psychological health outcomes. This is where you come in. Of course, there will be times in every family when teenagers are uncommunicative and withdrawn. At such times having a trusted adult outside the family to whom they can talk will make a big difference.

I'M NO GOOD
I'M THE BEST THING SINCE SLICED BREAD
LET'S HAVE A COFFEE AND A SANDWICH
THAT PROVES IT

Chapter 3
Depression

Anyone who has lived with teenagers for even a nanosecond knows that from time to time they can be down in the dumps, irritable and hard to live with. In most young people, these moods may last for a few hours or days, and may result from some loss or disappointment, or may occur for no apparent reason. However, when your teenager has a pervasive sense of despair that lasts longer than two weeks and interferes with other parts of their everyday life, such as work, school or relationships, they may be suffering from depression. This illness is much more than sadness – it is a relentless hopelessness that leads your teenager to lose interest in most of their usual activities and in some cases can cause them to want to die.

Normal stresses can seem unbearable for someone suffering depression, and indeed, the strain of soldiering on, or trying to pretend that 'nothing is wrong' can exacerbate the illness. If a young person is depressed and does not know it, they may resort to self-medication with alcohol and other illicit drugs, which may result in a substance abuse disorder, academic problems and even legal problems.

Prevention is all about good communication and persistent parenting. Not talking openly about depression means that the illness can remain hidden and untreated for years. As mentioned earlier, young people with depression usually do not receive treatment and care for five to fifteen years!

The national depression initiative, beyondblue, estimates that there are 160 000 young people with depression living in Australia and while there is no clear sex difference in childhood, in adolescence, girls have twice the rate of depression that boys in most Western communities do. This escalates during early adulthood and then somewhat diminishes – but still remains significant – in later years.

Depression can occur by itself, but is very often associated with other mental problems, such as anxiety disorders, obsessive compulsive disorder, anorexia and psychosis.

Types of depression

Researchers and clinicians have identified a number of different types of depression.

Unipolar disorders

In this type of depression an individual experiences depressive episodes only – so there are no highs, only lows. Clinicians usually break this depression into further subgroups.

Melancholic or endogenous depression is biological and associated with low energy, poor concentration and slow or agitated movements. It's relatively rare and responds well to antidepressant drugs and electroconvulsive therapy.

Non-melancholic or reactive depression is by far the most common type of depression and is often linked to stressful events in a person's life and to personality type.

Dysthymia is a chronic, low-grade depression that continues for many years, but with occasional periods of remission that never last more than a month or two. Sufferers may go on to experience major depression.

Bipolar disorders

Bipolar disorder (once called manic depressive illness) involves periods of mania interspersed with depression. In a manic phase, people are suddenly confident, optimistic, elated, excitable and uninhibited, but then usually fall into a black depression. Such states can also be accompanied by psychotic symptoms, such as delusions and hallucinations, where the young person is seriously out of contact with reality.

Cyclothymia is characterised by mild and alternating mood swings of elation and depression occurring over a long period. Because the mood swings are mild, and the elation enjoyable, people don't often seek medical help. The periods of elation and depression can last for a long period, such as a few months. Often, a person with cyclothymic disorder has a relative with bipolar disorder, or they may develop bipolar disorder themselves.

Seasonal affective disorder (SAD)

SAD is a subtype of mood disorder where there is a seasonal pattern of mood variation. Depressive symptoms usually start up in autumn/winter, and go into remission in spring/summer. The symptoms of seasonal affective disorder are atypical of depression, often comprising hypersomnia (needing to sleep all the time), carbohydrate cravings, increased appetite and weight gain.

Hannah's story

Hannah Marie Modra was just 17 years old when she took her life. The second-oldest of Mark and Ellen's five children, she grew up in a loving family in a normal house in a normal suburb, yet her family now live with the agonising question of what, if anything, they could have done to prevent the devastating loss.

Like all families, the Modras have had their fair share of trials and tribulations. Their eldest son, Luke, is profoundly autistic and was moved to a special accommodation centre four years ago, and Ellen was diagnosed with and survived breast cancer.

Photo albums show Hannah enjoying a happy childhood and adolescence, albeit impacted by the problems of having an autistic older brother. She loved singing, playing the piano, making cards, writing stories and keeping a journal. She was a voracious reader, avid exerciser (especially hiking, cross-country running, table tennis and swimming) and a Cats supporter.

As a big sister she shared her time equally with all her siblings, listening to music and having heart-to-heart chats with sister Clare, helping younger brother Joel with school and homework, and playing sport and games with Paul.

Along with the rest of her family, she had a deep spiritual faith, regularly attending evening youth services at her local church and teaching and helping children at Sunday school. She earned extra money by babysitting and working part-time at Subway. She loved going to the movies and parties and zipping off to the beach with friends. This solid base of warmth, friendship and love should have been a potent and positive amulet, a countervailing force against future unhappiness.

The day she died, Hannah, a straight-A Year 12 student at a state secondary college, had walked up on stage, accepted her prefect's badge and then fainted from (it is suspected) sheer physical exhaustion. She'd been driven home at lunch time by a teacher from the school.

The last few hours of her life were spent writing in her diary, chatting to friends on MSN and surfing the Net. When the rest of her family was home she had a conversation with her mother in the kitchen: 'Mum, I feel bad. I collapsed at school today – in front of everybody. I feel really really tired. I feel sad.'

Her mother suggested she have a lie down, and that she would ring the school to find out what happened. Hannah went upstairs and wrote the following entry in her diary:

Fainted at school today. At the front of assembly. Hardly slept last night. Survived a jog this morning with Dad, barely. I feel bad! There's no real reason I can think of. Lack of sleep maybe. Tomorrow is school camp. What is going on with me? Felicity Peel is nice to me. So is Shayaga, Ben and everyone. Today is the first day of Year 12. I haven't finished my holiday homework and I don't want to. Most people managed to finish all their homework. I feel like I can't do anything! But I can! I just don't want to! I don't want to bring down my whole school's score! I'm not excited about sport. I'm dreading house swimming and house athletics. Is it just 'cos I'm tired? It wouldn't be that hard to just end everything.

The next time Ellen saw her daughter, she was dead. She had inflicted a fatal wound and died within seconds.

Only the day before, Ellen had taken Hannah to a local doctor because she'd been complaining of sleep disturbance and lethargy. The young GP saw her for ten minutes, suspected anaemia and ordered some blood tests. That night, Hannah wrote in her diary:

> *I went to the doctor just then. Is something wrong? I dunno. I look in the mirror and I look so sweaty, pale and sick. Maybe it's just my imagination. Holiday homework AARGH! I feel so strange right now. I don't know what I want to do, except sleep. If it would help I would beg God to take me away. I don't feel like me. But I am me. And I've felt this way many times before, mostly quite a long time ago. I think it was two years ago. If it's my body's cry for help I want, really badly, to help it. Will I ever look healthy again?*

They say everyone is a genius in hindsight, and looking back, Hannah did show signs of depression. In the previous few weeks she'd told both parents that she was feeling unwell and sad, prompting the trip to the GP. She had also exhibited some uncharacteristic behaviour – she'd stopped cooking and helping around the house, things she used to enjoy. She had also been experiencing serious sleep problems: having trouble falling asleep, waking during the night and waking very early in the morning. As a result, she also repeatedly complained of being tired and having no energy. She'd also become overly self-critical, and had developed a preoccupation with past failures and mistakes, remarking to her parents and in her diary that she had let her friends down.

Importantly, there were also significant risk factors at play. Firstly, there was a family history of depression on both sides of the family, which undeniably ratchets up the chances for the next generation. Secondly, there had been a major change in the family when, four years earlier, her autistic brother (to whom she was greatly attached) had moved into a special accommodation facility. At the same time she had had to deal with the fact of her mother's breast cancer.

With such hindsight, it is almost certain that Hannah Modra suffered from rapid onset unipolar depression, a severe illness that distorted her moods, incited uncharacteristic behaviour, destroyed the basis of her rational thought and finally eroded her desire to live.

Despite Hannah's Herculean efforts to maintain an outwardly brave face, she had reached a point where she no longer found anything interesting, enjoyable or worthwhile. Everything that was once sparkling in her life now seemed flat. Over the last few weeks of her life, every thought, word and movement became an effort. Unbeknown to those who adored her, her depressed brain did little more than torment her with a dreary litany of her inadequacies and shortcomings, taunting her with the desperate hopelessness of it all. Without the reinforcements afforded by antidepressant medication and cognitive behavioural therapy, thoughts of death became her constant companion. Yet she gave few outward signs, other than complaining to her parents of feeling desperately sad and indescribably tired.

For Hannah, dying might have seemed the only release from the unbearable misery and overwhelming sense of inadequacy and blackness that surrounded her.

So what might have saved Hannah Modra? If her depression had not set in so rapidly and severely and her symptoms had not been masked by holiday distractions perhaps a sharp-eyed teacher might have noticed her decline and ordered an assessment. Or if she had not seen depression as a test from God and hidden her struggles she might have shared her worries with a pastor at her church. In an ideal world, Hannah, her family and her doctor would have realised what was happening to her. They would have talked openly about depression together so that she did not feel the awful burden of having to fight the disease alone. She would have gone to a youth-friendly empathic doctor, received a thorough and considered assessment, been referred to a specialist and would have received regular counselling, medication and frequent check-ups.

But circumstances conspired against her. In her own words Hannah wrote:

> *Depression, like abuse, needs to be talked about more. Fear of embarrassment and pride are both keeping me from the medication and counsellors.*

Her story stands as my inspiration for this book and should be a clarion call to families and all health, education and welfare workers to do their utmost to raise the emotional literacy of young people and their parents. Early recognition and help-seeking can only happen, as beyondblue says, 'if young people and their support network know about mental disorders, the type of help available and where to access help.'

Signs and symptoms of depression in teenagers

So what should family members and friends be looking for? What are the telltale signs? Parents should look for a cluster of the following symptoms that extend over a few weeks or more:

- avoiding school and friends (e.g. not returning calls)
- decline in academic performance
- increased irritability, anger or hostility
- indecisiveness
- absence of energy and motivation
- overeating or loss of appetite
- disturbed sleep (insomnia or hypersomnia)
- restlessness, agitation, disruptive behaviours, overactivity
- increased sensitivity to failure or rejection
- a sense of needing to be punished
- helplessness about being able to change the way they feel
- complaints about headaches, stomach aches, tiredness, 'growing pains'
- persistent sadness and bouts of crying
- gloomy and dark thoughts, and statements (direct and

indirect) that they feel worthless, self-critical, pessimistic about their future or don't want to continue living
- deliberate self-harm
- inappropriate risk-taking (e.g. inappropriate sexual contacts, reckless driving)
- drug and alcohol abuse
- uncharacteristic behaviours such as stealing and bullying.

Often young people with depression also experience constant worry (anxiety), which can cause physical symptoms such as stomach aches, headaches, back pain and heart palpitations. (See Chapter 6 for more on the relationship between anxiety disorders and depression.)

Risk factors for depression

There are lots of things that can put a young person at risk of developing depression, such as:

- problems at school (e.g. not coping with the academic

workload, not fitting in or being the victim of school or cyber bullying)
- unresolved grief over the death of a parent, sibling or close friend
- ongoing conflict or violence at home
- end of a relationship
- family break-up
- drug use
- alcohol abuse
- suffering a long-term illness or injury.

The causes of depression are complex. Yet sometimes it seems to occur for no apparent reason – in other words, there seem to be no current life events to explain its sudden onset. For this reason it is often more helpful to consider 'risk' versus 'protective' factors rather than focusing on causes.

Maintaining our mental health is a delicate balance and research suggests that this will rest on our underlying genetic predisposition. For example, children of parents with depression have a higher *risk* of suffering depression, but this does not mean they *will*. In the same way that your own father might have cardiovascular disease and you have a higher risk of getting it, you won't necessarily have a heart attack if certain protective factors are in place (no smoking, moderate drinking, good diet and exercise). So for young people at risk of developing depression, there are protective factors both external and internal (personal) which will reduce the risk and the balance will be maintained.

There is evidence to show that external factors such as exposure to family or community violence, chronic poverty, child physical and sexual abuse, bereavement, parental divorce or separation and substance abuse may tip the balance for a young person and may lead to them developing depression.

Similarly, personal risk factors may also tip the balance, with particular personality types (such as pessimistic people for whom the glass is always 'half-empty' rather than 'half-full') having a greater risk of developing depression. Poor interpersonal skills, coupled with negative thought processes, can also create difficulties for adolescents negotiating changing relationships with peers and families, searching for autonomy while trying to fit in, and simultaneously trying to succeed in a competitive academic and social environment.

In young people, depression is more common in girls than boys, so being female is a risk factor. The cause of the striking rise in the incidence of depressive symptoms in adolescent females is as yet unknown, but hypotheses include the influence of female gonadal hormones, psychological changes that accompany puberty and changes in social roles including the early sexualisation of young women. (See the introduction for a discussion of these.)

But the good news is that all these risk factors can be offset by protective factors such as social connectedness, life satisfaction and the acquisition of coping skills – all of which help to protect our young people (and us!). Martin Seligman, the father of positive psychology, says that if we can teach children aged 10, 11 and 12 optimistic thinking we can halve their rates of depression and anxiety as they go through adolescence.

Diagnosis and treatment of depression

It can be tricky to diagnose depression in young people because they:

- all have mood swings from time to time
- are highly motivated not to share thoughts and feelings with adult carers
- have a particularly strong sensitivity to control
- often don't have the emotional vocabulary to convey how they are feeling.

If you suspect your son or daughter may be depressed, the first step is to make an appointment with a GP (see Chapter 4 for more on this). Your doctor can then refer your teenager to a psychiatrist or psychologist if necessary.

While there is no blood test for depression, there is the K10 (Kessler Psychological Distress Scale) questionnaire, which is widely used as a straightforward measure of psychological distress. The K10 is in the public domain and is promoted on the beyondblue website. The numbers attached to the patient's ten responses are added up and the total score will range from 10 to 50. People who score:

- under 20 are likely to be well
- 20–24 are likely to have a mild mental disorder
- 25–29 are likely to have moderate mental disorder
- 30 and over are likely to have a severe mental disorder.

This is a screening instrument which allows GPs to make a clinical judgement as to whether a young person needs treatment. Taking a K10 to an initial appointment with a GP is a great start.

There are now many ways to treat depression, including talking therapies (such as counselling, cognitive behavioural therapy and psychotherapy) and antidepressant medication. If the burden of the disease is severe (self-harm, strong family history, withdrawal from friends, family conflict or school refusal) then a combination of medication and talking therapies will be used. See Chapter 5 for more on these treatments.

The National Health and Medical Research Council recommends cognitive behavioural therapy (CBT) as the first-line treatment for young people, as studies show that it is as successful as, or even more successful than, medication in helping them overcome mild depression. CBT helps in several ways:

- The counselling element helps ease the pain of depression ('you are not alone'), and addresses the feelings of hopelessness that accompany the illness ('we can fix this together').
- It helps the young person to identify unhelpful and distorted beliefs and unrealistic expectations, and teaches them to challenge them and replace them with more adaptive cognitions.
- It helps the young person recognise which life problems are critical, and which are minor.
- It helps them to develop positive life goals, and a more positive self-assessment.

Long-term recovery

After treatment for depression most young people get back to normal quite quickly. The problem is that they can very easily slip back into depression if another adverse life event comes along and diverts them from the developmental tasks I talked about in Chapter 2.

Relapse rates for depressed teenagers can be as high as 50–70 per cent, depending on which study you read, which means there is always a possibility of it recurring later in life.

To reduce the chances of a relapse, your son or daughter should get adequate rest, food and exercise, maintain social connectedness and do things that give them life satisfaction.

Healthy eating

Although there are no studies to prove that a particular diet can cure depression, there is evidence that having insufficient omega-3 fatty acids is associated with depression. Many studies have shown that societies with diets high in omega-3 fatty acids (found in anchovies, mackerel, salmon, sardines, tuna, flaxseed and nuts) have a much lower prevalence of major depressive disorders (including bipolar disorder and postnatal depression) than societies with very little omega-3 in their diets.

Alpha-linolenic acid is another type of omega-3 fatty acid and is found in flaxseed, canola oil, soybean oil, walnuts, and dark green leafy vegetables.

Protein-rich foods (such as turkey, tuna and chicken) are rich in an amino acid called tyrosine. Tyrosine boosts levels of the brain chemicals dopamine and norepinephrine. This boost can help young people feel more alert and makes it easier for them to concentrate.

Vitamin D (from the sun) increases levels of serotonin in the brain, but no-one is sure how much vitamin D is ideal. It seems it depends on where you live, the time of year, your skin type and your level of sun exposure. Research undertaken at the University of Toronto has shown that people suffering from depression, particularly those with seasonal affective disorder, experienced a reduction in symptoms as the levels of vitamin D in their body increased. The researchers recommend that we get about 600 international units (IU) of vitamin D a day from food if possible.

Exercise three times a week

According to beyondblue, keeping active is a key strategy in managing mild depression. Research shows that regular physical activity significantly reduces the risk of depression and that people who are physically inactive are more likely to have depressive symptoms compared to exercisers.

Regular aerobic and strength training activities of light to moderate intensity can result in up to a 50 per cent reduction in symptoms of depression and anxiety.

Promote sleep

An inability to sleep (insomnia) that lasts over a long period of time is also an important clue that someone might be depressed. (A small percentage of depressed people, approximately 15 per cent, oversleep, or sleep too much – this is called hypersomnia.) Lack of sleep alone cannot cause depression, but it does play a role. Lack of sleep caused by another medical illness or by personal problems can make depression worse.

Following are some ways to help teenagers improve the

quantity and quality of their sleep:

- Encourage them to go to bed and wake up at the same time each day to establish a rhythm.
- Make sure the bedclothes are not too hot, and the room is not overheated.
- Dim the lights in their environment 90 minutes before they go to bed.
- Keep the digital clock pointed away.
- Encourage them to learn relaxation and deep breathing techniques (such as listening to a relaxation CD).
- Make sure exercise is several hours away from bedtime.
- No caffeine, alcohol or nicotine in the evening.
- Use the bed only for sleeping – no lying in bed to watch TV or to read. This way, their bed becomes a cue for sleeping, not for lying awake.
- Get them to grab a pad of paper and scribble down anxious thoughts as a way of clearing their minds.

Meditate and relax

Meditation has been shown to be effective for an enormous range of physical and mental conditions, including heart disease, chronic pain, skin disorders, depression, anxiety, panic disorder and substance abuse disorders. It does this partly by reducing people's reactivity to stress and boosting their positive moods, self-esteem and sense of control.

Preliminary research suggests that the regular practice of yoga, too, may be an effective way to raise levels of the neurotransmitter GABA and to reduce symptoms of anxiety.

Communicate

Teachable moments arise every day through sharing the experiences of families or friends, reading newspaper stories, listening to the radio, surfing the Net and watching films, DVDs, and TV shows. Any suicide to which young people are exposed – however tangentially – needs to be reframed as the outcome of a mental illness (most often depression).

Talking about depression as an illness ensures that we take

away any stigma. If there is a family history then frank, open conversations about increased risk and discussions of protective factors are crucial. If you or your parents had it, share your experiences – it can set a positive example and open up the lines of communication between you.

If appropriate, discuss with your teenager what the early signs of their depression were, so that he or she will be more alert to a recurrence. Also, encourage your teenager to talk through their problems with a trusted adult. If possible, have them keep in touch with their therapist for a few months after feeling better.

TANDBERG
WE TOLD OUR DAUGHTER, "WAKE UP TO YOURSELF," "GET OVER IT," "STOP INDULGING YOURSELF! . . . NOTHING SEEMS TO WORK

Chapter 4
What can I do?

Before we take a closer look at anxiety and other mental illnesses, I want to take you through the things you can do to help, and what you can expect from our healthcare system in the process. The good news is that most of these problems are treatable and early diagnosis and prompt treatment is associated with a much better outcome. Yet astonishingly, 70 per cent of young people with mental and emotional problems *never* receive treatment for their illness, and of those that do, the delay between the onset of illness and treatment is usually from five to fifteen years.

One young man I met had suffered for years with undiagnosed depression, which caused him to have few friends and perform very poorly at school. He self-medicated with marijuana and eventually dropped out of school after being expelled for dealing drugs and was then kicked out of home. Homeless, his drug use escalated to other drugs and he eventually developed a drug-induced psychosis. This is what can happen when a mood disorder is not treated. Had his depression been picked up earlier, his trajectory might have been very different.

Parents and caregivers *must* play a key role because most young people, even those without a mental health problem, have a relatively poor understanding of their mental health needs and a lack of knowledge about available health services or how to use them. Many have enormous difficulties expressing their concerns. In addition, most young people will feel self-conscious about being asked personal questions, and will generally defer treatment until crisis point. Most commonly, they appear in the GP's surgery reluctantly, dragged along by parents or other caregivers.

Talking with your teenager

If you are worried about a son or daughter, the first step is to open up the subject for discussion. As young people come close to adolescence, peer relations and 'fitting in' become a priority.

It is normal for them to question the boundaries laid down by adult carers and to look to friends and the media for clues on how to behave. Robust disagreements can occur as the adults try to respect their offspring's mounting desire for autonomy and independence while still ensuring their physical and emotional safety.

In the olden days we used to sit around fires and tell our children stories, passing on information and wisdom and creating a bond that in most instances lasted a lifetime. Sadly, many of us decide we are too busy to do this now, and so our children grow up in emotional silos where friends, schoolteachers, Wikipedia and YouTube become their chief sources of wisdom.

Communicating with teenagers can be difficult, especially when the teenager is irritable, withdrawn, confused or anxious. However, even if we have made errors of judgement in our dealings with teenagers up to now, it is never too late. A good place to start is by acknowledging mistakes and resolving to address them. A teenager is much more likely to believe you when you say you are willing to listen, understand and help if you first admit to past misjudgements.

According to Paul Swets, author of *The Art of Talking with Your Teenager*, hearing is not listening. And in the same vein, talking is not always communicating. The words you use account for only 7 per cent of the message impact. Your tone of voice accounts for 38 per cent of the message impact, and the way you act while speaking (the nonverbal messages you send) accounts for an incredible 55 per cent of what your listener will believe.

To encourage a young person to communicate, you need to show an active interest in almost anything and everything they are involved in, from their music to their computer games. As Professor Greg Whelan says, 'If you can't talk to kids about their music how will you talk about sex and drugs?' Parents need to set aside time to ask what their teenagers think and feel about a variety of subjects.

The use of 'I' statements instead of 'you' statements can be a great help. For example: 'I'm disappointed you didn't come home when you said you would last night. This is the third time you've done this.' Rather than, 'You never do what I ask you to do! You make me so mad! You are so irresponsible!'

Effective listening requires empathy and knowing when to listen. Some tips for effective listening are:

- Care enough to make a solemn effort to understand.
- Maintain eye contact (unless you're in a car!).
- Focus attention on what is being said rather than what you are going to say next.
- Listen for thoughts and feelings, as well as facts.
- Think of questions to ask and ask them.

Remember, if you want your teen to talk to you, you need to invest in your relationship. Your investment of time with your teen will pay many dividends: you'll develop a genuine relationship with him/her and have an opportunity to influence their development into happy, healthy adults.

When is a good time to talk?

Teenagers are sensitive to control and the best conversations are ones that can occur naturally as opposed to the lecture or state-of-the-nation-style speeches often favoured by adults.

Don't try to talk to your teenager when they are:

- angry
- inebriated or drug affected
- with their friends
- on the computer or playing a video game
- on the phone or listening to an mp3 player.

The truth is that for adolescents, friends are hugely important and most parents teeter on the edge of obsolescence. Don't let chances for conversations go by. Grab moments you are in the same place at the same time with them. These are precious. The best times to initiate a chat include:

- While doing stuff together, such as fixing a motorbike, cleaning a car, cooking a barbecue, setting the table, or doing some garden chores. Conversations during these activities can be more open because they don't trigger sensitivity, seem more natural and can have less of a confrontational feel to them.
- While you're in the car together. Teenagers listen to everything you say even if they don't look like they do. Car talks

are adolescent-friendly because they take place in neutral territory, as opposed to talks in their room, where some may feel that their personal space is being invaded. Also, the diminished eye contact while sitting side by side allows the conversation to flow more comfortably and naturally.

- At sporting events or other regular activities. Accompanying a young person while they participate in activities they enjoy is a good opportunity to convey support, interest and pride. Concerts, awards nights, school or club events are all not-to-be-missed chances to demonstrate your care and concern.
- During down-time. Times teenagers are most likely to be resting and just hanging out are ideal opportunities to talk, catch up, and simply make an available time for both of you to bond.

How can I raise the subject?

Sometimes, so much water has flowed under the bridge that it is just too hard for the adults or the young person to sit down for a heart-to-heart chat, but thankfully, such situations are the exception rather than the rule. In such cases, indirect communication can be an effective technique for raising sensitive issues. Writing a note, a letter, an email or even a text message can break the ice. You may need to give them time to absorb what you are saying without having to respond to you.

Below are other ways to open a dialogue:

- Ask them about their usual out-of-school activities, and if they are still enjoying them. Also ask them whether their coach, trainer, music teacher, drama teacher etc. would notice if they had lost interest.
- Check out websites together such as those of youth beyondblue, Reach Out, or MoodGYM, and ask your teenager what they think about them.
- Ask them to play the interactive computer game ROC (www.reachoutcentral.com.au) and discuss the scenarios and how

they'd manage them in real life.

- Check out sites like Myspace and talk about some of the angst and suicidal blogging and what they would do if they were feeling the same way.

What if they won't talk to me?

If you are not confident to discuss your teenager's problems with them, you are not alone. As mentioned in the Introduction, an Australian Childhood Foundation report revealed that 60 per cent of parents believed they could be better parents and 75 per cent believed parenting did not come naturally. More than half of the parents surveyed lacked confidence in their parenting and 80 per cent wanted more information about parenting but were too afraid to ask for advice for fear of being stigmatised as a poor parent. If you feel this way you might benefit from a one-off session with an adolescent psychologist or a parenting class.

You could also start by utilising another parent, a family doctor, a school counsellor, or a school coach. Research shows that one of the most important people in the lives of some teenagers is their best friend's mother, so you could always word them up and ask them to approach your son or daughter.

The Reach Out website has a wealth of information written for young people, including several fact sheets on how to help a friend who is depressed or suicidal. If you know your teenager would resist your suggestion that they check it out, you could:

- ask them to tell you what they think of it, or to review it for you
- get their school to promote the site
- encourage another adult who they respect to mention it to them
- leave the web page open on the computer.

I remember listening to an interview with the friends of a girl who had committed suicide and hearing that the girl had often discussed dying with them, but that the friends didn't know what to do about it. While peers could theoretically play an important role in encouraging help-seeking behaviour, ignorance, stigma and a fear of being perceived as different are all major obstacles to them doing so. There is also the problem that failed attempts to help a suicidal peer might leave the young people vulnerable to trauma and stress.

Raising the emotional literacy of young people is a key goal for mental health professionals, and websites such as www.reachout.com and www.youthbeyondblue.com play a very important role.

Seeing a GP

If your teenager is showing signs of depression (as discussed in Chapter 3), or has other symptoms of mental instability, the next step is to see your family doctor or general practitioner. GPs in Australia see approximately 2 million young people under the age of 25 annually, representing over 11 million consultations. They are truly the backbone of adolescent mental health in Australia.

Given that GPs act as a gateway to the healthcare system and can facilitate access to other health and support services, a GP consultation is a vital first step in resolving mental health problems. According to Australian research, young people themselves perceive GPs as one of the most credible sources of health information.

All parents should, when their son/daughter hits puberty, encourage their GP to hold a special 'rite of passage' consultation, where the GP is encouraged to give the young person their own separate Medicare card. The GP should show the young person that with all future consultations, they will have their own separate, private file. Furthermore, they should explain the 'duty of care' when it comes to confidentiality. This means that all teenagers are by law entitled to privacy. However, there are exceptions to this if the young person is being harmed, harming themselves or intending to harm someone else.

Parents should not be frightened by this confidentiality. Doctors know that one of the best resources a young person will ever have is their parents, and most will encourage young people to tell their parents what is troubling them, even though this may be the goal of a future consultation. The most important thing is for the young person to have someone who they feel they can talk to, especially about sensitive issues such as mental health.

Confidentiality is crucial, as adolescents can be extremely embarrassed about discussing sensitive issues such as sexuality, substance use or other emotional problems, and are overwhelmingly concerned about being different.

Moreover, despite viewing GPs in a positive light, many young people believe that GPs treat only physical ailments and are unaware that they may be able to help them with emotional and psychosocial concerns as well. Research suggests that young people often go to GPs for relatively minor complaints. The three most common reasons young people see a doctor are for respiratory, skin and musculoskeletal conditions. Yet the main causes of adolescent morbidity illness are psychosocial and behavioural (unsafe sexual practices, binge drinking, illicit drug use, drink-driving, self-harm) and this discrepancy highlights the fact that young people frequently don't go to GPs for the problems that are really bothering them.

Why doesn't my teenager want to go to the doctor?

Young people face huge psychological, administrative and financial barriers in accessing GP services. Dr Fredericke Veit is a medical practitioner and researcher I worked with at the Royal Children's Hospital's Centre for Adolescent Health. She and her colleague Dr Lena Sanci have identified five main obstacles to young people visiting their family doctors:

1. **Lack of confidentiality.** Teenagers are worried that the doctor and reception staff will disclose information to their parents, friends or school, and are also concerned at the lack of privacy in the waiting room.
2. **GP's attitude and communication style.** Young people are concerned that the doctor may have unsympathetic, authoritarian and judgemental attitudes. The GP's approach and communication style will greatly influence how comfortable the young person feels about confiding their problems. GPs who comment on a non-medical aspect of the young person, such as their T-shirt, inquiring how their football team went on the weekend or even asking them the name of their

favourite band and who take the time to talk about confidentiality will help put the young person at ease.

3. **Formality.** Young people may feel intimidated by an overly formal clinic and waiting room, which can make them less willing to use the service again.
4. **Reception staff.** Teenagers can also be put off by the appointment booking procedures and the perceived lack of sensitivity and awareness of reception staff.
5. **Waiting times.** Lastly, the clinic opening hours and long waiting times can lead young people to give up on healthcare altogether.

For young people who wish to see a GP without their parents' knowledge, there are further barriers. Most young people do not understand the Medicare system and very few have their own Medicare card. As a result, many will have extraordinary difficulty meeting the costs of medical care, especially when practices do not bulk bill.

Encouraging a teenager to visit a GP

If your teenager is reluctant, you could negotiate a deal with them (and the GP) that if they do not like the GP they only have to stay for five minutes and then they can leave.

You could also warn the GP in advance that your teenager is anxious about attending and send a fax or email detailing the problem. This minimises the GP's data-gathering time so they can focus on the young person's wellbeing.

If your teenager is willing to discuss their problems with a professional, then choose an appointment time when they're well rested, well fed and not preoccupied with an important upcoming event. There is no point in taking them to the doctor if they are hung-over, high or too tired. If necessary, just reschedule.

While some teenagers like to have their parents with them, others do not. The most useful strategy is to offer them a choice. Some will appreciate an assurance that you will not go into the clinic room with the GP so that they have complete privacy

If your teenager refuses point-blank to attend, the best alternative is for you to go instead. On the basis of this, it is sometimes possible for the GP to arrange a phone consultation, a home visit or a virtual consult via email or msn.

Making the most of the visit

Prior to the appointment it can be very helpful to send a brief email to the GP outlining your specific concerns about your teenager's behaviour. This way you won't need to discuss them in front of your teenager, and you are free to leave the room and allow your teenager some privacy. The email can note briefly:

- when the mood disturbances or worrying behaviour occurs
- how long it's been occurring
- what seems to trigger it
- what circumstances make it worse/better
- whether your teenager is engaging in any alcohol or drug use.

It might also be extremely useful to bring along to the appointment a file containing any school report cards, previous professional evaluations such as psychological reports and a list of previous or current medications including over-the-counter and prescription medications, vitamins and herbal supplements that your teenager might be taking. Once again, you can simply hand these to the receptionist or post them to the doctor ahead of the appointment time.

How to find a youth-friendly GP

Unfortunately, not all GPs are comfortable seeing young people and some may lack the confidence, knowledge and skills to communicate effectively with them. The other major problem is time. A comprehensive screening of a young person is very difficult when there are thirty people in the waiting room. Many GPs are also unaware that they can obtain greater remuneration for longer consultations – which is often essential for young people with mental health problems.

Ultimately, this means parents will need to 'shop' around for a youth-friendly GP, one that has a 'developmental' perspective and an established reputation for being user-friendly, both in the way they run their consultations and also in the running of their practice. There are several ways to find a good GP:

- Ask student welfare personnel in your local school to direct you to the youth-friendly GP of choice in your area.
- Check out the organisation 'headspace', which is run by the National Youth Mental Health Foundation. There are thirty centres for young people around Australia. Simply go to its site and click on the Australia map to find the headspace centre closest to you.
- Try beyondblue's online directory of medical and allied mental health practitioners. Click on the Find a Doctor link to find someone appropriately trained in your area.

You'll know you've found a good GP when they go out of their way to establish a supportive and trusting relationship with your teenager. A youth-friendly GP will:

- Attempt to see your teenager alone, where appropriate
- Offer both verbal and written assurance about confidentiality
- Educate them about their rights
- Create a separate medical file for them
- Show them how they can apply for their own Medicare card

- Take a history, conduct a sensitive physical examination and order any tests needed
- Explore beyond the presenting complaint, even if it is relatively minor
- Use standard assessment tools such as a HEADDS interview to screen for the balance of risk and protective factors in their life (home, education/employment, activities, drugs, depression, sexuality). This may take place over several appointments.
- Offer information about risk behaviours and how to protect themselves
- Work with the family to educate you about the changes your adolescent is going through and engage you where appropriate in taking an active role in any treatment or management plan
- Encourage teenagers who have a strained relationship with you to eventually discuss their issues with you (knowing that adult caregivers can potentially be one of the young person's greatest resources). This may not be a realistic goal in an initial consultation, but may be possible at a later date.

What happens next?

If you have private health insurance, your GP can refer you to a private specialist treatment centre. If you don't have insurance, you can get a referral to the local services provided by your state or territory government.

The public system

Child and Adolescent Mental Health Services (CAMHS) provide a range of programs for infants, children and young people and exist in one form or another in each state and territory. A GP can refer your son or daughter to a CAMHS. They give priority to those in greatest need and specialise in working with those children and adolescents experiencing severe and complex problems and disorders that cause high levels of distress, disability and risk of harm.

Usually the young person is seen by a CAMHS intake worker and a history is taken by a psychologist, social worker, occupational therapist or nurse. Depending on the urgency of the problem and how busy the service is, an appointment is made, and this can takes some days or weeks.

After an initial visit, families are given a case worker who will arrange subsequent visits. Staff turnover, however, can be quite high so there is a danger that the young person might not always see the same professional.

Private treatment

In the private system, waiting times are likely to be shorter and there is less staff turnover, so your son/daughter is more likely to be seen by the same professional all the time.

Your GP should have a list of psychiatrists and psychologists in your area who are trained to work with adolescents, and will be able to refer you to one.

Psychiatrists

Adolescent psychiatrists are in high demand and one of the most poorly distributed of all health professional groups, so it can be hard to get an appointment. There is nothing stopping you from approaching the psychiatrists yourself and securing an appointment – although once secured you will still need a GP's referral.

Visits to psychiatrists are eligible for Medicare rebates, though you will still need to pay the gap, which can be anything from $15 to $90 or more.

Psychologists

To find a psychologist, ask a youth-friendly GP, or check out the beyondblue and headspace sites. There may also be a psychologist based at your place of study or work, or at your local community health centre. You don't need a referral to see a psychologist, unless you are accessing the government's care plan (see below). Parents can also call the beyondblue info line (1300 224 636) or look in the Yellow Pages under psychologists. The Australian Psychological Society (www.psychology.org.au) also provides a Find a Psychologist service.

If you (or your teenager) are a Medicare card holder, there are a number of Australian government initiatives under which you are able to claim rebates for visits to a psychologist. To receive psychological services under Medicare, a person must be referred by their GP or in some instances by a psychiatrist or a paediatrician, and must have a diagnosable mental disorder. These include psychotic disorder, schizophrenia, bipolar disorder, phobic disorder, anxiety disorder, adjustment disorder, depression, sexual disorder, conduct disorder, post-traumatic stress disorder, eating disorders, panic disorder, alcohol use disorders, drug use disorders, sleep problems, attention deficit disorder, obsessive compulsive disorder, co-occurring anxiety and depression and bereavement disorders.

Dementia, delirium, tobacco use disorder and mental retardation are not regarded as mental disorders for the purposes of the new mental health Medicare items.

All psychology Medicare services are limited to a maximum of twelve individual sessions per client per calendar year, with a review by the doctor who referred you required after the initial six sessions. In addition, you will also be eligible for twelve group session services, where appropriate, in a calendar year.

The cost to you and the rebate available from Medicare will vary depending on the length of the session, the type of psychologist consulted (general or specialist clinical) and the fee being charged by the psychologist. If the psychologist decides to bulk bill then you will not have to pay anything. However, if the psychologist does not use the bulk billing method then you must pay the difference (the gap) between what they charge and the Medicare rebate. This will vary and you must confirm this with the psychologist before commencing your treatment.

If you happen to have private health insurance, you cannot use ancillary (extras) cover to cover the gap. Information on rebates can be found on the Australian Psychological Society website (www.psychology.org.au/medicare/psych_medicare_items/).

Emergencies

If a teenager has refused to discuss their problems with anyone (including a GP) and their behaviour is life-threatening, then parents have to show granite-like resolve. This approach involves remaining calm (often in the face of provocative and distressing behaviour) and telling the young person that if they choose to be violent towards themselves and others, then you have no choice but to call the local Crisis Assessment Team, police or ambulance.

Tell them that they can do what they want when they are 18, but until then you are their legal guardian. Further, inform them that you are concerned about their welfare and that they can either choose to see a professional or go to the police. Be a broken record – those are the *only* choices. Be strong and remain the rock they need in their life. But this is going to be hard work, so get some backup from friends or relatives.

All mental health practitioners should help you develop an emergency plan, especially when you are dealing with adolescents experiencing severe and complex disorders that cause high levels of distress, disability and risk of harm. The contact numbers of these services should be placed within easy reach or better still typed into your mobile phone for one-touch emergency dialling.

Crisis Assessment Team (CAT)

Each major health region in Australia has a Crisis Assessment Team, or CAT team, usually staffed by a mix of nurses, social workers, psychologists and psychiatrists. They mostly work a rotating roster of three eight-hour shifts in teams of four or five at a time, depending on the size of the hospital to which they are attached.

These teams, which number over twenty in Victoria alone, were first developed by the director of the Alfred Hospital's psychiatric unit, Associate Professor Peter Doherty, in 1987. These triage teams go under different names in each state or territory. For instance in Queensland they are called Community Assessment and Treatment Team (CATT). Whatever their title, CAT teams were a key element of the newly de-institutionalised mental-health system, and were intended to remove the stress from public hospitals by creating a mechanism to assess acute young patients in their own environments and admit only the most desperately ill to beds. The reality is that these mobile troubleshooting teams have become the frontline of mental health care in many states and territories, and unfortunately the demand on such services is so astronomical that some parents call the CAT teams the 'Can't Attend Today' teams.

If a parent calls a CAT team, they will initially be put through to a psychiatric triage service over the phone, which will assess the urgency of their situation. CAT teams are not armed and do not have powers of entry or restraint, but sometimes families find it difficult to know whether to call the police or the CAT team. A shift of psychiatrists into private practice and a lack of new recruits have also left many teams without appropriate medical cover. Now 80 per cent of calls for help are referred elsewhere.

Sometimes a family who is getting nowhere with the CAT team and yet harbours real concern for their teenager might be better off heading for the nearest accident and emergency ward, where at least there is a better than even chance that an assessment by a psychiatric registrar can be made.

Emergency help lines

Lifeline

13 11 14 (cost of a local call)

www.lifeline.org.au

Longstanding 24-hour telephone counselling service. Also

provides information and referrals for people with mental-health problems. See also the Resources section at the end of this book.

Kids Helpline

1800 55 1800 (free call from land line)

www.kidshelp.com.au

Kids Helpline offers free confidential 24-hour telephone counselling services for five to eighteen-year-olds in Australia. On the Kids Helpline site, young people can email a counsellor or chat to one online between 3 p.m. and 9 p.m. Queensland time, Monday to Friday and 10 a.m. and 4 p.m. Queensland time, Saturday.

HEALTHY BODY
HEALTHY MIND
I DIDN'T REALISE THERE'D BE SIDE EFFECTS

Chapter 5
An overview of treatments

Thankfully, young Australians with a mental illness now have more treatment options available to them than at any other time in history. Psychological treatments are particularly effective for treating the most common mental health conditions such as anxiety and depression and are the treatment of choice for most child and adolescent problems. The evidence suggests that they tend to be more helpful than medication over the long term, with less chance of relapse. I have listed the treatments here so that you will be familiar with them when I mention them later in the book.

Psychological treatments

Often referred to as 'talking therapies', or simply 'therapy', these treatments help young people change the way they view themselves and their various 'worlds' (family, peers, school and the wider world), particularly how they react to challenges and adversity. Talking with a psychologist, counsellor, psychiatrist, social worker or other qualified healthcare professional can help them to make sense of their feelings and experiences, which in turn enables them to interact more meaningfully with others and allows them to begin to enjoy their normal activities again.

Traditionally, counselling was performed face-to-face in confidential sessions usually in an office, between the therapist and client. However, these days counselling is often conducted by telephone, in writing and via internet chat sites like msn, or even video conferencing.

Some people are unclear about the difference between a psychologist and a psychiatrist. Psychiatrists have a medical degree, which involves up to six years of studying general medicine, followed by further study to specialise in psychiatry. They can prescribe medication and often combine medication with other forms of psychological therapy.

Psychologists study human behaviour in their undergraduate and postgraduate degrees before undertaking a few years of supervision prior to gaining full registration. While they do not have a medical degree (and are therefore unable to prescribe medication), many study for a similar number of years to specialise in various aspects of psychology. All psychologists are legally required to register with the Psychologist Registration Board in their state or territory. In addition, those who register with the Australian Psychological Society (APS) have undertaken further study (totalling six and eight years) and are recognised by the following letters after their name:

- Hon FAPS (Honorary Fellow of the Australian Psychological Society)
- FAPS (Fellow of the Australian Psychological Society)
- MAPS (Member of the Australian Psychological Society)
- Assoc MAPS (Associate Member of the Australian Psychological Society)

Adolescent psychologists are experts in human teenage behaviour. They not only specialise in treating young people with a mental illness, but also address everyday adolescent problems such as school stress, learning difficulties, relationship troubles (both family and peer), risk-taking behaviours including drug and alcohol abuse and chronic illness.

A further differentiation can be made between counselling and clinical psychologists. Counselling psychologists are usually trained in a wide variety of basic therapeutic skills, while clinical psychologists are typically focused in one or a few areas (e.g. anxiety disorders, substance abuse). Counselling psychologists can and do specialise, but their training is more general. Counselling and clinical psychologists can treat the same kind of patients and the overlap between the two fields continues to grow.

Cognitive behavioural therapy (CBT)

CBT helps a young person to recognise negative thought patterns and behaviours and to replace them with positive ones. It can quickly bring about important changes to a person's daily life and outlook for the future. It is based on the theory that our thoughts and beliefs have a major influence on the way we feel – that irrational, unhelpful, negative or self-defeating thoughts can trigger anxiety and, over time, lead to anxiety disorders and depression.

The purpose of CBT is to help the young person challenge negative thinking and to establish new thought patterns, skills and habits. It is a structured therapy which involves a partnership between the psychologist and adolescent. The young person is fully involved in planning the treatment, with each session involving discussion, explanation and the practice of skills. Often the young person will be given 'homework' between sessions where they have to practise a particular technique.

Interpersonal therapy (IPT)

Interpersonal psychotherapy is a short-term supportive therapy that grew out of the interpersonal psychoanalysis work of Harry Stack Sullivan, who believed that interpersonal factors contribute heavily to psychological problems. IPT was originally developed as an individual therapy for adults, but was subsequently modified for use with teenagers.

Depressed and anxious young people can be derailed by the

innocent remarks of family or friends and often perceive criticism where none was intended. IPT seeks to help teenagers learn how to deal with others more effectively so that instead of being caught up in a web of damaging misinterpretations and rejection, young people can minimise the amount of conflict in their lives and obtain assistance from adult carers and peers.

IPT looks at the ways in which a young person's current relationships and social context cause or maintain symptoms rather than exploring other deep-seated causes of the symptoms.

Psychodynamic therapy

The aim of psychodynamic therapy is to help young people find relief from their emotional pain, and is based on the classical psychoanalytical theory that this pain results from unconscious motives and conflicts. However, psychodynamic psychotherapists do not necessarily accept Freud's view that these unconscious motives and conflicts are ultimately sexual in nature.

This form of therapy is usually long-term and looks at how childhood and earlier life experiences affect how the young person thinks and acts now. It has been found to be particularly helpful in treating generalised anxiety disorder and phobias first experienced in childhood.

Sessions may be scheduled from one to three days per week, with greater frequency allowing for more in-depth treatment. The duration of individual sessions varies but is typically 45–50 minutes. It is not usually possible at the outset of treatment to estimate the number of sessions that will be necessary in order to achieve the person's goals.

After a course of psychodynamic psychotherapy has been completed, the teenager should, in general, continue to cope better with life conflicts, have better interpersonal relationships and be more productive at school.

Dialectical behaviour therapy (DBT)

DBT, developed by Marsha Linehan at the University of Washington, is a type of psychotherapy that aims to help people learn and apply skills to cope with strong emotions, such as those associated with bipolar disorder. The skills are:

1. **Mindfulness meditation**, where people learn to observe, describe and participate in all experiences (thoughts, sensations, emotions and things happening externally in the environment) without judging them as 'good' or 'bad'. This is the key skill that underlies all the others.
2. **Interpersonal effectiveness**, where people learn to successfully assert their needs and to manage conflict in relationships.
3. **Distress tolerance skills**, which involves learning to accept and tolerate distress without doing anything that will make the distress worse in the long run (e.g. engaging in self-harm).
4. **Emotion regulation**, where patients learn to identify and manage their emotional reactions.

Acceptance and commitment therapy (ACT)

This treatment stresses the young person's acceptance of their internal experience, while maintaining a focus on changing behaviour and psychological flexibility. Instead of teaching them to better control thoughts and feelings, ACT teaches them to just notice, accept and embrace these private events.

ACT employs six core principles to help young people develop psychological flexibility, including stepping back and observing thoughts and feelings without getting caught up in them or running from them, as well as setting goals and taking action to achieve them. Research suggests that when delivered by an experienced practitioner, ACT can be highly effective.

Medication

Most young people diagnosed with a serious mental illness are offered medication to help them manage their symptoms, at least in the first instance to give the psychological treatments the opportunity to work. Understanding their illness and what to expect from the medication empowers the young person to achieve greater personal control over their illness and its symptoms.

Depending on factors such as the severity of the illness, the type of medication, and the teenager's age and gender, the efficacy and side effects of medication can vary. For most of the illnesses described in this book, medication usually takes a number of weeks to reduce symptoms.

Antidepressant medication

Though not well understood, depression is associated with an imbalance of certain brain chemicals, including the neurotransmitters serotonin (5HT) and norepinephrine (NE). These neurotransmitters act as messengers between parts of the brain, or between the brain and the body, and insufficient amounts result in the symptoms of depression. Antidepressants slow down the re-absorption (reuptake) of neurotransmitters, and relieve the symptoms of depression.

Over the years, scientists have developed several kinds, or classes, of antidepressant medications. Older classes (developed in the 1950s) are the tricyclics and monoamine oxidase inhibitors (MAOIs). Newer classes of antidepressant medications include selective serotonin reuptake inhibitors (SSRIs) and serotonin noradrenaline reuptake inhibitors (SNRIs), and generally have fewer side effects. These medications may have different effects on different people, and many people may try more than one before they find one that works for them.

There is some evidence of increased suicidal thoughts (although not of actual suicides) and other side effects in young people taking antidepressants, so SSRI antidepressants are generally not recommended for paediatric use. However, the National Institute for Clinical Excellence has stated that fluoxetine (brand name Prozac) can safely be used for those under 18. Sertraline (brand name Zoloft) is the only other SSRI approved for paediatric use, but only for children and adolescents with obsessive compulsive disorder.

Note: When the time comes to stop *any* antidepressant medication, the drug must be withdrawn slowly under a doctor's supervision.

Minor tranquillisers

Benzodiazepines (Valium, Ducene, Serepax, Xanax, Kalma), known as 'benzos', work very quickly to calm young people down. They are used in the treatment of anxiety, insomnia, generalised anxiety disorder, phobias and panic disorders. However, their effects do not last long, and prolonged use carries a risk of physical dependence and may interfere with cognitive therapy. Because benzodiazepines slow down the workings of the brain and the central nervous system alcohol should not be consumed as it increases the sedative effect of the medication.

Beta blockers

Beta blockers (sometimes written as ß-blocker) are a class of drugs primarily used in the management of cardiac arrhythmias but are also used to treat anxiety. Beta blockers can alleviate heart palpitations and stop hands from trembling as they block adrenaline receptors in the heart and muscles. Because they prevent the feedback that provides cues for anxiety they are used for performance anxiety, stage fright or transient exam-related anxiety.

They may also be helpful for blushing and sweating. Typically these drugs are consumed about an hour before a feared event and last a couple of hours.

Anti-psychotic medications

Medications used to treat psychosis are known as antipsychotics (or sometimes major tranquillisers or neuroleptics). Usually taken on a daily basis as a liquid, tablet or wafer, or as a long-lasting injection (called depot), they work by changing the chemicals in the brain (such as dopamine) that are causing the psychotic symptoms. A teenager experiencing psychosis for the first time (first-episode psychosis) will usually be required to stay on their medication for a year, but if they relapse they may be expected to take it for much longer.

There is a variety of antipsychotics. When deciding which one to prescribe the psychiatrist will take into account factors such as the adolescent's symptoms, other medications being taken and possible side effects. They are usually classified into two different groups: atypical and typical. (See Chapter 12 for more on these.)

Ritalin

Ritalin (generic name methylphenidate) and Attenta (dexamphetamine) are psychostimulant medications used for the treatment of attention-deficit hyperactivity disorder (ADHD). These drugs act by balancing the brain's neurotransmitter chemicals. Such drugs can only be prescribed by psychiatrists and paediatricians. Dosage is usually daily (two or three doses) in tablet form and can be continued for months or years. (See Chapter 8 for more about this medication.)

I REMEMBER WHEN HE SPOKE HIS FIRST WORDS
I REMEMBER WHEN HE UTTERED A WHOLE SENTENCE

Chapter 6
Anxiety disorders

Many parents, myself included, like to romanticise their teenage years as a worry-free time and often project this fantasy onto their teenage children. Mums and dads often rationalise that their teens should be out having fun, playing sport and making friends – just like they allegedly did! However, for increasing numbers of young Australians life is not so simple. The Australian Bureau of Statistics reports that 13 per cent of young people experience anxiety, transforming normal, happy young people into highly anxious individuals who have difficulty breathing every time they go out in public, and may not even be able to attend school, not just for a day or two, but for months or even years.

An anxiety disorder, which is what psychologists call any anxiety that interferes with your daily life, is one of the most common mental illnesses in Australia, affecting 20 per cent of us. Yet in 2006 research by the Anxiety Disorders Alliance showed that 61 per cent of us have little or no knowledge about these illnesses. This lack of awareness is demonstrated by the fact that up to 98 per cent of young people who experience depression have actually had a pre-existing anxiety disorder that contributed to the onset of the depression. Often the anxiety disorder goes undiscovered, with symptoms of depression being the first symptoms reported to general practitioners. Below are some other important statistics:

- Teenage girls are affected twice as often as boys.
- Anxiety disorders occur most frequently among those aged 18 to 25.
- Only 28 per cent of young people with anxiety disorders get help.

Twenty years ago, anxiety disorders in young people were almost unheard of. This is partly because human beings actually need a certain amount of stress or arousal to motivate us to give our best performance. If approached in the street by a mugger, for example, the anxiety we feel (the 'fight/flight response') enables us to react quickly to protect ourselves. A manageable level of anxiety about end-of-year exams, or an upcoming race or sporting competition, has been shown to be useful in enhancing our performance.

Anxiety is a normal response to something terrifying or complicated. Adrenaline flows into the bloodstream, priming muscles, focusing attention, flooding the body with oxygen and releasing chemicals that transform the sugar in the bloodstream into energy. This fight/flight response happens to everyone faced with a difficult situation. However, for some teenagers this anxiety is all-consuming and is triggered by experiences that some might consider quite ordinary or manageable.

Susan's story

Susan, a 20-year-old student at a local TAFE, had been experiencing moments of sudden, absolute panic every week for several months. During these episodes her heart pounded; she trembled; her mouth got dry and she felt as if the walls were caving in. The feelings only lasted a few minutes but when they happened, the only thing that seemed to relieve her fear was walking around her house and reminding herself that she was in control. She was so afraid of having another attack that she stopped riding in cars unless she was driving (so she could be sure she could stop the car if necessary). She only went to TAFE if she found an aisle seat in the back row so that she could leave quietly if she had another attack. She avoided any situation in which she might have felt out of control or embarrassed by her own terror. Susan was suffering from panic disorder.

She finally went to see a student counsellor at the TAFE who referred her to a psychologist. She was given information about her anxiety, taught relaxation techniques, and received cognitive behavioural therapy. She went on to complete her diploma and start a relationship. She still occasionally has panicky thoughts, but knows she can control them using the techniques she learned.

Risk factors for developing anxiety disorders

Anxiety disorders respect no boundaries. They can strike families whether they are rich or poor, married or divorced, urban or rural. Research suggests that in at least half the cases the cause can be attributed to genetics. Finnish scientists have recently identified genes that may predispose people to developing anxiety disorders when triggered by stressful life events. Beyond that, different triggers can be found in different cases. Anxiety may be generated by a bad experience in the past such as a severe loss or trauma (e.g. a car accident, getting trapped in a lift, being attacked by a dog), leaving the young person anxious every time they encounter a similar or identical situation.

Typically in young people an incident at school, such as an episode of being bullied, can trigger anxiety. Substance abuse, be it alcohol, marijuana or amphetamines, can also exacerbate symptoms of anxiety.

Signs and symptoms of anxiety disorders

Although the disorders have different symptoms, they all tend to make the teenager withdraw into themselves in an attempt to avoid situations or objects that trigger the anxiety. In early adolescence sufferers may avoid social interaction with their peers and even with their family. In later adolescence, they may avoid getting involved in relationships because they fear rejection, and can develop serious self-esteem problems. Untreated, such young people will struggle at school and are less likely to achieve their educational potential, which in turn affects their job prospects. Teenagers with untreated anxiety in particular are likely to suffer co-existing conditions such as eating disorders and drug and alcohol problems. But the problem affects entire families. As with any case of illness, siblings may be resentful of the attention the sufferer is getting.

Contrary to popular belief these adolescents aren't overindulged hypochondriacs; they are suffering a mental disorder that can make their lives a living hell.

Symptoms can be both physiological and psychological.

Common psychological symptoms include:

- fear
- intense apprehension
- unbearable tension
- uncontrollable worry
- calamitous thought patterns (e.g. where they assume a catastrophe is just around the corner).

Such thoughts ratchet up the fight/flight response described earlier, resulting in a range of physical symptoms, including:

- nausea
- chest pains
- involuntary shaking
- increased sweating
- breathlessness and difficulty breathing
- racing heart.

The experience of panic and overwhelming anxiety is perceived as being so profoundly awful that it may lead many teenagers to simply avoid circumstances, places and situations that they associate with the attack, and can over time lead to agoraphobia (see later in this chapter).

Types of anxiety disorders

There are many different types of anxiety disorders, each with their own symptoms and treatments. I have included the most common ones here, along with their symptoms. Note that I have discussed obsessive compulsive disorder (OCD) in a separate chapter because it is one of the more prevalent types.

Generalised anxiety disorder (GAD)

This is an extreme, uncontrollable anxiety that cannot be attributed to a specific event or object and occurs for the majority of the time (more days than not) for more than six months. It is different from occasional serious worry that doesn't noticeably lessen quality of life.

Signs to look for include restlessness; difficulty concentrating or sleeping; irritability; fatigue; and muscle tension, which can cause jaw-clenching, trembling and twitching. Other symptoms include headaches, irritability, sweating and hot flashes. Some young people report feeling light-headed or out of breath, while others feel nauseated or have to go to the toilet frequently. Others say they feel as though they have a lump in their throat.

GAD is emotionally and physically exhausting. When someone worries about doom and gloom being just around the corner day-in and day-out over a lengthy period, they constantly feel tired and rundown, and can be inattentive and distracted in social situations, even with people who are emotionally close to them.

Specific phobias

A specific phobia involves an intense, all-consuming and uncontrollable fear of a particular object or situation accompanied by intense anxiety. If you even talk about the object or situation that scares them, they may have a panic attack, and they will go to extremes to avoid the object or situation, thereby reinforcing the phobia.

A phobia is more than just a powerful distaste for certain

places or things; it is an intense fear response which is out of proportion to the actual place or thing. There is no need to worry if a young person 'hates', say, spiders or sharks or heights. The key is how powerful their feelings are, and whether they can handle them. Parents should be on the lookout for teenagers who are forever inventing elaborate ways to avoid particular objects or situations, expressing dread at the next possible encounter and saying that they know their fear is disproportionate but that they feel it is beyond their control.

There are many different kinds of specific phobias, including fear of heights, blood, needles, lightning, open water, rats, mice, spiders, sharks and even objects such as balloons and string.

Claustrophobia is a fear of enclosed or confined spaces such as lifts, trains or small rooms. People with claustrophobia fear having a panic attack if they are in such a situation.

Hypochondria refers to an extreme concern or worry about having a serious illness. People with hypochondria have a constant fixation with their body and with self-examining and self-diagnosing medical problems.

Social anxiety or social phobia

Young people with social phobia display an excessive and unreasonable fear of being the centre of attention for fear of negative evaluation from others. Teenagers who are merely shy can be distinguished from those with a social anxiety disorder by the intensity of their fear, the level of avoidance, and the disruption it causes in their everyday lives. Young people with social anxiety don't just feel nervous before giving a speech in front of a class, they worry about the speech for weeks or months beforehand, lose sleep over it and can have intense symptoms of anxiety during the speech such as a racing heart, shortness of breath, sweating, or shaking. The symptoms usually do not subside but remain severe or even worsen as the speech progresses.

People with social phobia realise that their fears are unfounded, but are still unable to control them. They will avoid any situation that could lead to scrutiny or evaluation such as social functions, being in a crowd or speaking to others.

Panic disorder

Panic disorder is the chronic fear of having a panic attack and is diagnosed when people who experience recurring attacks are frightened for a month or more of having another one. Some people may develop agoraphobia as a result of panic disorder.

A panic attack is an experience of acute anxiety, usually peaking within 10 minutes and complicated by hyperventilation and worsened by the fear of collapse or death. Such panic may occur in situations from which escape is not possible or help is not available, typically public transport, travelling alone, crowded or lonely places. This is quite different from intermittent episodes of intense anxiety in response to a real threat.

Panic attack symptoms include:

- palpitations
- chest pains
- sweating
- chills or hot flushes
- trembling

- shortness of breath or choking
- nausea
- light-headedness
- feeling of 'unreality'
- feeling one has lost control of mind and body
- feeling one is dying (often from a heart attack, stroke or brain tumour).

Agoraphobia

Agoraphobia is a fear of being in places or situations from which escape might be difficult or embarrassing if the sufferer has a panic attack. It often develops as a result of other anxiety disorders, such as social phobias (where people avoid social situations), post-traumatic stress disorder (where people avoid stimuli related to a particular trauma) and obsessive compulsive disorder (where people avoid obsessive thoughts). It usually leads to avoidance of certain places and situations.

Post-traumatic stress disorder (PTSD)

PTSD is a recurring, anxious reliving of a horrifying event (such as rape or a traumatic accident) over an extended period of time. It is marked by upsetting memories (flashbacks), 'blunting' of emotions, irritability or outbursts of anger, and difficulties sleeping. This is different from anxiety following a trauma that fades steadily over the course of a month or so.

If a teenager witnesses or experiences an event that caused or threatened to cause serious injury, they may develop the following signs and symptoms of PTSD up to six months after the event:

- avoidance of thoughts, feelings, activities or places associated with the event
- difficulty recalling details of the event
- anxiety symptoms such as irritability, jumpiness, difficulty sleeping, feelings of detachment from others, diminished interest in activities.

One way to treat PTSD is to gradually expose the person to the things that remind them of the traumatic event until they lose their power to disturb. This type of therapy is highly specialised and should only be carried out by experienced therapists. However, anxiety management strategies such as hyperventilation control or progressive muscle relaxation can all be taught by a family doctor.

Diagnosis and treatment of anxiety disorders

When the physical and emotional consequences of anxiety are unmanageable and are interfering with the day-to-day life of your teenager, your first port of call should be a visit to the doctor. Chapter 4 has advice on choosing a doctor and how to encourage your teenager to visit.

The most common form of treatment for anxiety disorders is cognitive behavioural therapy (CBT), which is described more fully in Chapter 5. CBT is usually undertaken with a psychologist trained in this method, although some psychiatrists also offer it. In some cases medication may be prescribed as a short-term measure, though research suggests that CBT is much more effective than medication in managing anxiety disorders in the long term. Thus medication typically takes the form of a short course of tranquillisers or antidepressants to help your teen deal with their symptoms while other treatment options are given an opportunity to work. In conjunction with CBT, the young person is educated about the nature of the disorder and may also be taught relaxation and structured problem solving techniques, be given graded exposure to the situations that precipitate anxiety, undertake regular aerobic exercise, and learn to monitor their moods.

It is important to start treatment as quickly as possible. Experience shows that the longer you leave an anxiety disorder untreated, the worse it gets. In severe cases of school phobia, for example, where a young person has been at home for several years, the success rate in getting them back to school is no better than 50 per cent.

Recognising the true cause of the young person's distress is the first step in the treatment of anxiety disorders.

I TRUST HIM,..
I NEVER LIED
TO MY PARENTS
BUT WHAT IF HE
TAKES AFTER ME?

Chapter 7
Obsessive-compulsive disorder

Close your eyes and try to visualise a teenage girl who takes up to twenty minutes to move from one room to another because she has so many rituals to perform to keep her fear at bay, or the boy so afraid of germs that he stops eating, literally starving himself, so that he doesn't have to face going to the toilet. Or the family that must wear rubber gloves when preparing food, as one of their members gets hysterical at the thought of contagion. These young people are suffering obsessive-compulsive disorder (OCD).

OCD is an anxiety disorder where young people are subjected to a bombardment of intrusive, irrational thoughts and fears (often about contamination or harm to self or others) to which they have learned to respond by engaging in a series of ritualised, repetitive behaviours such as washing, checking and re-checking. Some sufferers get so distressed that they hit or scratch themselves just to get some relief from these obsessive thoughts.

OCD shows up most often around puberty. Most teenagers have worrying thoughts from time to time, routines they follow, and things they like to do in a particular way, but when these thoughts or actions begin to affect your son or daughter's every-day life it's considered to be OCD.

Research suggests that 1–4 per cent of children and young people suffer from OCD. So in your teenager's secondary school of 1000 students, it is quite possible that at least 10 students have it.

Ryan's story

Ryan, now 26, was always an anxious child. His mother, Shauna, said that when he was about twelve he started having panic attacks and developed a host of phobias and rituals. He was terrified of contracting HIV. He traced over and over particular letters of the alphabet as he wrote. He covered himself in anti-septic and adhesive plaster. He checked, double-checked and triple-checked doors, windows and under his bed. He pulled the whole family into his world of repetition and anxiety.

'He was living in hell,' Shauna said. 'We all know what it's like to be anxious, but this was 100 times worse and for every minute of the day.'

Suspecting the disorder, Shauna contacted a support line and was sent a copy of Dr Chris Wever's book, *The Secret Problem*. After Shauna visited her doctor and was referred to a psychiatrist, Ryan was prescribed SSRIs for a period and underwent intense cognitive behavioural therapy, which involved exposing him, gradually and with support, to the things he'd become terrified of. He had to endure a lot of discomfort.

'It took four to six months to really see a difference,' Shauna said. 'It was a journey of lots of steps forward and lots of steps back. There's no magical finish to it. He's still anxious, but he says,

"Mum, I don't repeat, there are no rituals, there's nothing." He controls it now. It doesn't control him. He is working overseas, he has a long-term girlfriend and he has a happy life.'

Risk factors for developing OCD

Experts are not sure exactly what causes OCD, although it is often accompanied by a family history of the illness. Sometimes it occurs after an upsetting event such as the death of someone close. But like most anxiety disorders, OCD can affect any sort of person from any sort of background. The most important thing for families to remember is that it is no-one's fault!

Many older children have mild obsessions or compulsions, such as recurrent and undesired thoughts to harm others, rituals such as hand-washing, repeatedly carrying out meaningless activities such as placing objects in order or getting dressed in a certain order, but these usually disappear when they get older.

OCD as a condition usually begins before the age of 25 years and often in childhood or adolescence. In individuals who seek treatment, the average age of onset appears to be somewhat earlier in men than women: 9.6 years for boys and 11 for girls.

Signs and symptoms of OCD

Some teenagers describe recurring disquieting thoughts or images which they feel they have to 'block out' with compulsions or rituals. A common unwanted and intrusive thought seen in young people is that of contamination with germs, with the result that they constantly wash their hands.

Obsessions are:

- invasive and relentless thoughts, impulses or mental images that cause distinct anxiety or distress; not purely excessive worries about real-life problems
- always counterbalanced or repressed by the teenager with some other thought or action
- always seen by the teenager as creations of his or her own mind (not imposed from the external world).

Compulsions are:

- recurring behaviours (e.g. hand-washing, ordering, checking) or mental acts (e.g. praying, counting, repeating words silently) that the person feels motivated to perform in response to an obsession
- aimed at preventing or reducing distress or preventing some feared event or situation
- unconnected in any realistic way with what they are designed to counterbalance or prevent.

Most young people occasionally have similar thinking patterns; however, the difference for OCD sufferers is that the thoughts and behaviours exert almost complete control over their lives. Most people with OCD know that their obsessions are irrational, but are powerless to prevent them.

Once they have performed the ritual they will feel a temporary relief, but such feelings are transitory and the thoughts often manifest again quite quickly, compelling the young person to repeat the ritual once more.

Diagnosis and treatment of OCD

The formal diagnosis of OCD needs to be made by a psychiatrist or other mental health professional. A GP can refer your son or daughter to such a specialist. The key is to form a team with your family doctor to find someone who has expertise in this area, who takes a good history and is thorough about diagnosis.

If diagnosed early, young people with OCD responds well to treatment. Psychiatrists recommend a combination of CBT and medication. Two SSRIs (fluvoxamine and sertraline, sold as Luvox and Zoloft) have been approved for the treatment of children with OCD and attract a rebate under the Pharmaceutical Benefits Scheme. In milder cases CBT alone may be sufficient.

According to Chris Wever, a child and adolescent psychiatrist in private practice, 'Counselling, relaxation therapy, hypnotherapy, diet, all those sorts of things that are seen as less intrusive, gentler – there is no evidence they work for OCD.' Wever is also Associate Professor at the Faculty of Health Sciences and Medicine at Bond University and the author of *The Secret Problem*, a book about OCD in children and teenagers. '[It] needs to be treated early and treated as well as possible the first time so the kid has a sense of mastery and control over it, they are the boss of it, it's not the boss of them. The longer it's around, the harder it is to treat.'

Wever and his colleague Dr Sloane Madden say children diagnosed with the disorder tend to fall into one of three categories: those who get better; those for whom it sometimes comes back but who manage it well; and those who have to work hard to manage it consistently.

Children likely to have a tougher time of it include those who:

- develop severe symptoms very early
- develop severe tics
- develop eating disorders
- self-medicate with drugs and alcohol
- are 'always arguing with authority figures'.

The family, the therapist and the child need to form a united team against the disorder, which can be particularly challenging with a highly oppositional child.

I WAS WORRIED LAST WEEK THAT HE WAS LACKING ENERGY
SLAM!
TANDBERG

Chapter 8
ADHD

Someone once said teenagers have the attention span of a border collie, and they're not far wrong. As a result of the cerebral cyclone of teenage brain development, almost all young people tend towards the messy and chaotic from time to time – prone to making spur-of-the-moment decisions and often shooting from the lip. Because of the adrenaline coursing through their veins, teenagers can also become restless when forced to sit still for extended periods. This is all fairly normal.

So what constitutes excessive distractibility or disorganisation? When does difficulty paying attention and excessive energy become attention-deficit hyperactivity disorder (ADHD)?

Given the headlines of the past decade, attention-deficit disorders often seem like the 'diagnosis du jour' for almost every child who wagged school or daydreamed in class. But real ADHD is no faddish syndrome – it is a complex illness first identified by Dr Frederick Still, a British paediatrician, in 1902, whereby a young person experiences constant difficulties listening to others and following instructions.

According to the National Institute of Mental Health in the USA, somewhere between 3 and 9 per cent of the world's population endure the condition, with more than 60 per cent of these being young people. In Australia, the National Survey of Mental Health and Wellbeing found that 12.3 per cent of boys and 3.8 per cent of girls aged 6 to 17 had ADHD.

Many parents of children with ADHD wonder whether or not their child will have it forever. Australian research suggests that approximately 80 per cent of people diagnosed as children will continue suffering from the condition as teenagers, and 70 per cent of teenage sufferers will take the disorder into adulthood. For most young people, the symptoms diminish as they get older.

Yet a diagnosis of ADHD does not take away from a young person's natural talents. In my experience, young people with ADHD are some of the brightest, most creative, intuitive, imaginative, passionate and sympathetic people you would ever meet.

With effective treatment, these young people can make the most of their skills and the vast majority become productive, law-abiding citizens.

Some of us now think that many famous achievers including Albert Einstein, Orville and Wilbur Wright, Thomas Edison, Pablo Picasso, Louis Carroll, Eleanor Roosevelt and Louis Pasteur had ADHD, but they also transformed the world. If your teenager has been diagnosed and is upset, show them this list and look up their achievements together on the internet. Ask your son or daughter to consider what our world would be like if these people had never dared to dream!

Jordan's story

Jordon at 15 years of age could not be still for a nanosecond. He rushed through life, even though he seemed not to know what direction he was headed in. His household chores were either not done at all or completed under duress at lightning speed.

His marks at school were terrible – within seconds of the start of a class he would become distracted and begin annoying his friends. He could not follow instructions, interrupted his teachers when they were speaking and found it impossible to focus. His parents fought each night as they pleaded with Jordon to do even a bit of his homework, which was usually impossible because he'd left the required material at school, or it was buried beneath the dirty clothes, CDs, gum wrappers and chip packets on his bedroom floor. Whatever he handed in was usually full of errors, omissions and obvious mistakes. He was even dropped from his football team as he'd failed to front up for practice on five occasions.

Jordon was referred to a psychologist who conducted some psychometric testing and diagnosed Jordon with ADHD. He was referred to a behavioural paediatrician who prescribed a psychostimulant. Although initially reluctant to put their son on drugs, Jordan's parents agreed to a three-month trial. Within a week the school noticed significant changes in Jordon's behaviour and he reported that he was able to concentrate, focus and perform at school. He remembered his books, became more organised and even restored some order to his room. At the time of writing, the improvement in his academic performance, behaviour at home and school continues to be exceptional.

Risk factors for developing ADHD

Multiple studies of families have revealed that ADHD has a strong genetic link. Approximately 80 per cent of young people inherit the condition from their family. If one parent or a sibling has ADHD, additional children have about a 30 per cent chance of inheriting it, which increases to 50 per cent if both parents have ADHD.

Environmental factors also play a part. Maternal smoking of cigarettes, drinking alcohol during pregnancy, problems at birth and head injury have all been implicated in about 20 per cent of young people who acquire ADHD.

Yet despite what the tabloids would have you believe, ADHD is *not* caused by bad parenting or stressed-out families, though there is no question that adolescents with ADHD performed better when parents modified their home and used specific behavioural strategies that are helpful to these young people.

Being male is no longer considered a risk factor, either. Female sufferers struggle academically in the same way as boys do, it's just that their symptoms are less noticeable.

A recent study suggested that girls with ADHD may have a much higher risk of developing eating disorders as adolescents. This is because they already have impulsive behaviours that can set them apart from their peers, and as they get older, their impulsivity may make it difficult for them to maintain healthy eating habits, resulting in self-consciousness about their body image and the characteristic binging and purging.

Signs and symptoms of ADHD

A young person with ADHD will have a combination of the following:

- makes careless mistakes with schoolwork, at a job, or in other activities
- often appears not to be listening, even when directly spoken to
- is always disorganised or running late
- has a hard time maintaining attention until a task is completed or activity ended
- regularly misplaces important items or forgets commitments
- has trouble following directions
- is easily distracted by what happens around them
- avoids homework or any other task requiring thinking and problem-solving
- hates school.

British researchers argue that there are two types of ADHD: moderate and severe (also known as hyperkinetic disorder).

Moderate ADHD

The symptoms of hyperactivity, impulsivity and inattention occur singly or together at home, school and other settings and in multiple domains (for example, in achievement in schoolwork or homework). The illness prevents the young person dealing with physical risks and avoiding common hazards; prevents them forming positive relationships with family and peers and can stall the young person's development, including the formation of peer relationships, emancipating from adult carers, connecting with school and getting a job

Severe ADHD

The symptoms of inattention, impulsivity and hyperactivity are all present in multiple settings and multiple domains, and developmental impairment is so severe that the young person has significant difficulty maintaining relationships or obtaining (let alone retaining) employment. If their illness was undiagnosed in childhood, their academic performance may be poor. A lifetime of struggling with the disorder often means they will have very low self-esteem and resilience. In many instances, a young person with undiagnosed ADHD can be driven to self-medicate with illicit drugs or alcohol in an attempt to cope with their feelings of disappointment and failure.

Concurrent issues

It is very unusual to see someone with only ADHD. Most young people have another mental health issue as well. Sadly, rates of personality disorders and other psychological problems, such as anxiety or mood disorders, are high.

Learning disabilities are seen in almost half of young people with ADHD, including problems with oral expression, listening, reading comprehension and/or maths. Their behaviour also often results in anxiety and depression. More than a third of these young people have a condition known as oppositional defiant disorder, characterised by disobedience, disrespect for authority and antisocial behaviour. Teenagers with ADHD are also at risk of developing a conduct disorder condition characterised by aggression, deceit and delinquency. Successful treatment of ADHD is unlikely unless the co-existing difficulties are addressed as well.

Diagnosis and treatment of ADHD

Where a young person with ADHD has moderate levels of impairment, the British National Institute for Health and Clinical Excellence (NICE) suggests that parents are referred to a group parent-training/education program, either on its own or alongside a group CBT treatment program with their child or young person. These groups work on improving social skills with peers, problem-solving, self-control, listening skills and dealing with and expressing feelings.

In severe cases of ADHD, where school-age children and young people have not responded well to parent-training programs or group psychological treatment, the evidence indicates that psychostimulant medication such as methylphenidate (Ritalin) is moderately to highly beneficial.

Two long-acting forms of methylphenidate are available.

Ritalin LA (long-acting) has a duration of six to eight hours, while Ritalin Concerta lasts ten to twelve hours, which can be useful as it only needs to be taken once a day.

For 75 per cent of patients correctly diagnosed, psycho-stimulants can be very effective, making the young person feel calmer and more in control. Teachers are often the first to remark on changes, as students can focus and finish their work, some for the first time. The most common side effects include insomnia and loss of appetite. Some teenagers initially become irritable, teary and withdrawn, but these side effects are usually short-lived.

Many parents worry that drugs to treat ADHD are over-prescribed; however a recent New South Wales government review concluded that it is a myth that doctors have created a 'Ritalin generation' by over-prescribing drugs for children with ADHD. Only 20 per cent of ADHD sufferers were prescribed stimulants.

Parents who discover their teenage son or daughter is suffering from ADHD, particularly if no such diagnosis was obtained when they were in primary school, report mixed feelings. Some express a great sense of relief when they learn that they are not responsible for their offspring's behaviour, but also feel upset and guilty that the diagnosis was not made earlier.

A total ADHD treatment program should include:

- regular visits to a mental health professional
- parent education
- maintaining a regular schedule at home, in school, after school and on weekends
- building a support team that includes parents, teachers, instructors and coaches
- involvement in social skills groups.

Consistency is everything – the young person needs to know that the rules and consequences at home will also apply elsewhere.

MIRROR MIRROR ON THE WALL
WHOSE NOSE IS TOO BIG?
WHOSE BOTTOM'S TOO BIG?
WHOSE BREASTS ARE TOO SMALL?
WHOSE LEGS ARE TOO SHORT?

Chapter 9

Body dysmorphic disorder (BDD)

Young people with body dysmorphic disorder (BDD) are obsessed with a part of their body they believe is abnormal and makes them malformed or grotesque to look at. Their supposed imperfection causes great inner turmoil and anxiety, which can send their self-esteem plummeting. The psychological distress can be so great that it impairs both their occupational and/or social functioning, sometimes to the point where they shut themselves off from the world and live in complete isolation.

BDD is an equal-opportunity disease, affecting young people of all genders, social classes and ages. It is believed that between 1 and 2 per cent of Australians suffer from it, though estimates are difficult because sufferers always try to hide it. Previously known as dysmorphophobia, it usually begins in early adolescence.

Not surprisingly, people with this disorder make up about 15 per cent of patients who visit plastic surgeons, cosmetic dermatologists and cosmetic dentists. Research shows that there are high rates of depression and suicide among sufferers.

Richard's story

Richard was 15 when a girl in his class made a throwaway comment about his looks. It meant nothing to her but for him it was particularly painful, and started a series of events that would last for years. He became so convinced that he was ugly that he would walk with his head down or wear a hat with a large peak, and he confessed that if he could have worn a balaclava, he would have. Nothing his family or friends said made any difference, as he was convinced that they were just being 'nice' to him to save him from the cold, hard truth that he was in fact grotesque. He regarded all compliments as insincere. Richard would avoid mirrors or anything that offered a reflection. After two years, his mental state was such that he thought he was the most repulsive being ever to walk the earth, and that he must avoid inflicting his ugly self on others. Eventually he stopped socialising altogether and always came straight home after work and shut the door. Richard finally went to a GP, who referred him to a psychiatrist who treated him with a combination of medication (Zoloft) and cognitive behavioural therapy. Within a few months of treatment most of his symptoms had gone and he had enrolled in a TAFE course. At the time of writing, he is enjoying life.

Risk factors for developing BDD

No-one knows what causes BDD. Some experts point to genetics, others implicate environmental factors such as being abused or invalidated as a child. As with most mental health problems, the likely cause is a combination of nature and nurture. Some recent neuropsychological studies have found that MRI scans of BDD sufferers show an enlarged caudate (the C-shaped structure deep in the brain's core), while other studies suggest a malfunctioning of the brain chemical serotonin.

Another contributing factor might be our culture's preoccupation with physical attractiveness and youth. In 2008 a professor of psychiatry at the University of Melbourne surveyed first-year university students in Victoria and China for rates of BDD. He found that the young Australians were seven times more likely to suffer extreme and obsessive body image problems than their Chinese counterparts, and that gym junkies were the worst affected. Interestingly, Chinese-born Australians had the same high rate as Caucasians. Clearly cultural values play a part in explaining the stark difference.

Signs and symptoms of BDD

So how would you know if your son or daughter had this condition? Firstly, someone with BDD is 'obsessed' with their appearance – or usually one specific bit of their body. It may involve a small defect – like a mole or acne scarring – which to others may not even be noticeable. This exclusive focus can dominate their every waking moment, with some sufferers reporting that hardly a moment passes when they are not thinking about (or checking) the way they look and obsessing about the body part that they loathe.

Secondly, repetitive and intrusive thoughts dominate their consciousness and they may spend hours worrying about their appearance while covering mirrors and showering in the dark to avoid glimpsing the offensive part of their body. If they leave the house, they do so wearing psychological camouflage such as bandages on their faces, excessive amounts of make-up, large glasses, hats and baggy clothes. Camouflaging (reported by 94 per cent of sufferers) appears to be the single most common symptom among patients with BDD.

If your son or daughter persistently obsesses about their appearance or a part of their body – take note. Is this a one-off remark, or is this a pattern? It is not unusual for teenagers to have occasional worries and wobbles about their developing bodies, but BDD is different: it is a deeply distressing, unhealthy psychological fixation that profoundly interferes with their life, impacting on their school work, relationships and mental health.

Diagnosis and treatment of BDD

Diagnosis is often complicated, as young people with the condition are often too deeply embarrassed to discuss it with anyone, let alone a professional person. See Chapter 4 for tips on opening a dialogue with your son or daughter, and encouraging them to see a GP.

It is not unusual for doctors to prescribe antidepressant medication to BDD sufferers to decrease their obsession with minor or imaginary physical flaws and to reduce their compulsive behaviours. The medication allows the young person to get the most out of cognitive behavioural therapy, which has been found to be particularly helpful in teaching young people to challenge their beliefs about their appearance and to learn ways to cope so it doesn't interfere with their life.

If you suspect your son or daughter has BDD, in addition to ensuring they receive proper diagnosis and treatment, perhaps suggest they read some of the outstanding books listed in the Further Reading section at the end of this book. Reading about the condition can reduce the sense of isolation that many sufferers feel. It's also good to talk to other people in the same situation. Support groups can be found online at www.anxietyaustralia.com.au or through a hospital anxiety disorders treatment unit.

THE COST OF THE NINE MONTH STAY IS $53,000
DOES THAT INCLUDE MEALS?
TANDBERG

Chapter 10
Eating disorders

Anorexia nervosa (commonly known as anorexia) has the highest mortality rate of any mental illness yet is one of the most poorly understood. It is predicted that between 8 and 20 per cent of sufferers will die as a result of the disease – half of them by their own hand – and that a further 30 per cent will remain chronically ill for the rest of their lives, battling complications such as heart failure, osteoporosis, digestive diseases, chronic anxiety, psychosis and depression. Estimates are that one or two in every 100 young women and one in every 1000 young men will suffer from it.

Bulimia nervosa (known as bulimia) is an eating disorder characterised by episodes of binge eating followed by compensatory behaviours such as self-induced vomiting (known as purging), fasting, the use of laxatives, enemas and diuretics, and overexercising. It is estimated to be twice as common as anorexia – one in every fifty women and one in 500 men.

About 90 per cent of those who are known to develop eating disorders are female. It is most common in teenagers and young adults, though it can occur in children as young as 8 years old.

Cecilia's story

Fifteen-year-old Cecilia was a sporty, healthy student at a boarding school. She loved all physical activity and was frequently complimented for looking extremely fit. At that stage her body mass index (BMI) was 18.5, which is already low for a growing teenage girl. Although it was never mentioned aloud, a competition developed in one of the dormitories between the girls, as to who could lose the most weight. For competitive Cecilia, the urge to exercise became irresistible. She used to sneak out late at night and go for long runs, but at the same time ate less and less. This behaviour spiralled out of control and led to progressive weight loss and a reduction of her BMI to a life-threatening 14.7. When she returned home for the holidays, her poor physical and mental health led her parents to seek help and a diagnosis of anorexia with depression was made. She underwent psychological therapy and was given a meal plan under the supervision of a dietician. Despite prescribed restrictions on her physical activity and careful supervision and support from her parents, she continued excessive exercising, with inadequate food intake. Her deteriorating physical state resulted in her admission to hospital, where she gained weight over two weeks. She left hospital deeply upset by her weight gain and resumed excessive activity. She was clearly not responding to therapy.

Cecilia's family decided to try the Swedish Mandometer Method for 108 days (which included a period of inpatient care). During this time her intake of food and rate of eating both increased (and her perception of satiety decreased). With these months of normal eating and good nutrition, her psychiatric symptoms diminished and her physical state returned to normal. She has finished school and is now at university and has not relapsed.

Risk factors for developing eating disorders

Eating disorders are thought to be caused by an amalgamation of different factors, including cultural pressures, psychological issues, family environment and biological factors. These risk factors act together in different ways so that the road to anorexia is unique for each person.

In Australia, being slim is the standard of beauty for many young women and is often equated with success, happiness, and self-control. Teenage girls are assailed with messages from all forms of media, telling them to do whatever it takes to achieve a body shape that very few women naturally possess. However, this romanticised, wafer-thin body is totally incongruent with the inherited factors that decide most girls' natural body shape and size. This inconsistency leaves many teenage girls perpetually dissatisfied with their weight and figure. Is it a coincidence that in countries that do not correlate thinness with beauty, eating disorders are rare? Yet, virtually all teenagers are subject to this mass marketing and since only a small percentage develop an eating disorder, clearly this too cannot be said to be a prime cause of the disease.

Some young people who experience severe trauma (sexual assault or childhood abuse), endure abusive family situations or have difficulty making friends learn to regard their eating habits as one of the few aspects of their lives over which they have any control. Some clinicians also argue that some teenagers restrict caloric intake to avoid the sexual and social demands of adolescence.

Part of the challenge for clinicians is working out whether the traits that occur with an eating disorder are the cause or effect of it. Extreme weight loss itself causes known psychological problems including personality changes, depression, anxiety, mood swings, obsessive thinking, irritability, feelings of inadequacy and social withdrawal.

Signs and symptoms of anorexia and bulimia

Bulimia and anorexia are distinct illnesses, but they do have some similarities. For example, both appear most commonly in women and both tend to begin in the teenage years, although anorexia most often occurs around puberty, while bulimia occurs a bit later. Sufferers of both illnesses share the same fear, guilt and shame about food and weight gain, are undernourished and, as a result, may have dry skin, brittle hair and nails, be constipated, be sensitive to temperature changes and have irregular periods. Both may develop food rituals, like only eating certain foods or at specific times, and they may eat in secret.

Anorexia

The main criteria for the diagnosis of anorexia nervosa are:

- excessive weight loss or lack of normal weight gain, often to the point of starvation
- intense fear of gaining weight or becoming fat
- a seriously distorted image of body weight or shape
- the absence of at least three menstrual periods in a row in teenage girls (amenorrhea).

Other signs are:

- curious mealtime rituals, such as dividing food into minuscule portions, stirring food around the plate and discarding

or concealing food so it does not have to be consumed
- considerable increase in the time taken to eat, yet consuming very little
- circumventing opportunities to eat, missing mealtimes
- denying feeling hungry
- extreme focus on food, eating and body weight and shape
- continually weighing oneself
- inflexible eating patterns, such as excessive controlling of calories and fat even when underweight
- amassing recipes and preparing food for others while finding reasons to avoid eating
- accumulating or hoarding food
- wearing shapeless clothes to conceal the amount of weight lost, or to hide what they imagine to be their fat, ugly body
- feeling fearful or anxious before eating and guilty after eating
- grumbling about feeling bloated or full after eating a tiny amount of food
- having no interest in normal hobbies and activities
- socialising less with family and friends

- exercising obsessively
- having dry skin, thin hair that breaks or falls out easily and growing 'down-like' hair on body
- having problems sleeping
- feeling tired and lethargic
- feeling moody and depressed.

Without treatment anorexia can cause life-threatening health problems (heart trouble, kidney damage, seizures) and even death. Osteoporosis (the loss of bone mass) is widespread in anorexia nervosa resulting in a predisposition towards stress fractures and other bone abnormalities.

Bulimia

There are two types of bulimia nervosa: purging and non-purging. Purgers use self-induced vomiting and other ways to rapidly remove food from the body before it can be digested, such as laxatives, diuretics and enemas. They may also exercise or fast, but this tends to be a secondary form of weight control.

Non-purging bulimics (6–8 per cent of sufferers) use excessive exercise or fasting after a binge to offset the caloric intake.

Unlike anorexia, bulimia can be very difficult to identify because young people with bulimia tend to be of average weight (or only slightly above or below). Their eating and exercising patterns may not be as rigid, either, making it harder to diagnose.

Signs that your teenager may be binging include:

- eating large amounts of food within a small period of time
- alternating between overeating and refusing to eat
- evading any opportunity to eat in public
- concealing junk food around the house
- taking food from the kitchen
- hiding food wrappers in the rubbish.

Signs of purging include:

- frequent visits to toilet while eating or immediately after eating, often running water to cover up the sounds of throwing up
- a scent of vomit on breath, frequent use of air fresheners, strong mints, breath spray and gum

- regular use of diuretics and/or laxatives/enemas
- exercising obsessively, particularly immediately after meals.

Other signs of bulimia include:

- calluses on the knuckles, a byproduct of sticking fingers down the throat to induce vomiting
- puffy 'chipmunk cheeks' due to severe vomiting
- dental problems and mouth sores caused by frequent vomiting
- obsession with food and calories
- excessively self-conscious about weight and appearance
- poor self-esteem and negative body image
- increasingly isolated and withdrawn from family and friends.

With bulimia, the binge–purge cycle may be repeated several times a week or, in more serious cases, several times a day, causing serious medical conditions such as inflammation of the oesophagus, chronic gastric reflux, peptic ulcers and dehydration (from the frequent vomiting). Other common problems include electrolyte imbalance, which can lead to cardiac arrhythmia, cardiac arrest and even death. The repetitive insertion of fingers or other objects into the mouth and throat can causes lacerations to the lining of the mouth or throat. Frequent contact between teeth and gastric acid, in particular, may cause severe caries and the erosion of tooth enamel along with swollen salivary glands.

Diagnosis and treatment of eating disorders

Identifying anorexia is very difficult because most sufferers deny that they have a problem. Some may rationalise their overexercising by asserting that they want to be healthy and fit or to stay competitive in their chosen field of sport. Even those who are near death often still refuse food, rationalising their behaviour by pinpointing areas of their bodies that they believe to be overweight. If you notice some of the signs and symptoms described above in your teenager, try to get them to talk to you by telling them your concerns, naming the precise behaviours you have noticed. Psychologists recommend gentle persuasion over more punitive approaches. You need to accept that when your anorexic teenager looks in the mirror they do not see the same gaunt figure you see. Confrontation almost always triggers defensiveness and shuts down the very communication you are trying to encourage. Don't worsen the situation with rebukes such as 'You just need to eat!' or 'You are acting irresponsibly.' Instead try 'I' statements like 'I'm just so concerned about you', or 'I'm just so worried about you.'

The goal is to make the young person with the eating disorder aware there's a problem before it becomes severe, and to get them to talk to their GP. Offer to go with them to the appointment if they want you to, or respect their privacy if they don't. See Chapter 4 for more on encouraging this crucial first visit.

If they deny there is a problem or refuse to seek professional help, suggest that they talk with another trusted adult, such as an extended family member, teacher or spiritual leader. If the symptoms are severe, accountable adults *must* take responsibility in obtaining treatment, which is much easier if the person is a minor. Be sympathetic and tolerant, but firm. Dealing successfully with eating disorders takes time.

Once you have succeeded in getting your teenager to the doctor, the GP will usually diagnose an eating disorder if your son or daughter weighs 15 per cent less than they should for their height and age, and if they have particular beliefs related to their food intake, weight and shape. The doctor will ask about weight history, family problems, attitudes to food, dieting and weight loss, and about the way they look, or feel they should look. Diagnosis will also involve a comprehensive medical examination with blood tests and/or an electrocardiogram, which records the electrical activity of the heart over time.

Current methods of managing eating disorders in adolescents and young adults vary from one centre to another, and although many eventually have a favourable outcome, professional treatment involving family therapists, dieticians, psychiatrists, psychotherapists and physicians is often lengthy and very expensive, with a substantial risk of relapse.

A new method of treatment, developed at the Karolinska Institute in Sweden, takes a dramatically different approach to the treatment of eating disorders. Instead of searching for psychological causes, the program focuses on the disordered eating patterns of patients in the belief that many of the psychological symptoms that accompany eating disorders, such as obsessive-compulsive behaviour, excessive exercising, mood and anxiety disorders, are actually triggered by the young person being in 'starvation mode'.

Patients have daily one-on-one sessions with a case worker specially trained to help them eat from a plate attached to a scale (the 'Mandometer') that measures and displays the weight of their food and how fast they are eating in comparison to target rates. These targets are modified as treatment progresses. In the course of each meal, the young person is also asked to assess how full they feel during and after each meal, to teach them how to recognise normal feelings of satiety. After each meal, clients rest with a carer, in a warm room, or wear a heated jacket, which decreases the desire to exercise and reduces feelings of anxiety. In time, when a little weight is regained and eating behaviour has improved (i.e. eating rates have reached a certain level and eating rituals with negative effects on others have reduced), the young person progresses to eating with other clients in the clinic and eventually stops using the Mandometer.

According to figures from the clinic, duration of treatment varies from 9 to 14 months, with 75 per cent of patients in remission after this time. As well as addressing the consumption of food, the program provides long-term treatment designed to help the young person re-adapt socially.

The drawback of this approach is the cost – a nine-month treatment costs about $53 000. More information about this program can be obtained from www.mandometer.com.au.

TANDBERG

Chapter 11
Self-harm

You only have to walk down the road of any city in Australia to see that unprecedented numbers of young people are decorating their bodies with tattoos and piercings – tongue studs, multiple earrings, and rings in noses, belly-buttons, chins and eyebrows are now quite common. In such instances the motivation is clear: to assert identity, rebel against authority or fit in with a particular youth subculture. Apart from the aesthetic issues, parents have no reason to be concerned about their newly decorated teenager's mental health.

This is altogether different from young people who surreptitiously cut, scratch, burn or in some other way mutilate their body. In such instances, the young person is deliberately inflicting harm on themselves as a way of coping with overwhelming emotions.

While it is often hard for adults to understand, there is logic behind self-harm in young people. Rationales vary: some teenagers are believed to be hurting themselves when they feel under pressure, as if they are opening a valve to let off steam; for others self-harm is a coping mechanism. Some young people lack the vocabulary to express intense thoughts and feelings, so self-harm becomes a way of articulating difficult emotions (deep sadness, self-hatred, anger, loneliness and guilt). Many clients tell me that when they hurt themselves they feel a release which helps them to cope, albeit temporarily.

In Australia, as many as 12 per cent of all teenagers engage in self-harm, most of them young women, though the number of young men who harm themselves is growing. The harm is inflicted in a secretive manner and often continues for some time without anyone finding out. The most common forms I see include (in order of frequency):

- cutting
- burning
- taking overdoses of medicines
- swallowing harmful substances

- biting or hitting
- banging their body against hard objects
- pulling hair
- scratching and picking at sores.

Alice's story

Alice was 13 years old and had socialised with the same group of friends since she was quite small. There was one girl in the group who everybody admired and wanted to be like. Alice and her friends followed her everywhere and did only as she did. One day the girl decided to exclude Alice, and almost overnight, the whole group behaved as if Alice didn't exist. They didn't include her in anything and there were days when no-one even spoke to her. Alice was utterly overwhelmed and didn't know how to cope. She didn't talk to anyone about how she was feeling, and bottled up all the pain, hurt, anger, sadness and loneliness. The only thing that gave her temporary release was self-harm. Anything that happened, no matter how minor, seemed catastrophic to Alice and she felt she could only cope by engaging in yet more self-harm. Every night she would silently cry herself to sleep, overwhelmed by feelings of loneliness and sadness.

Finally, she went to see the school counsellor, who referred her to a psychologist. Initially, she found it very difficult to open up with a complete stranger, but as she got to know him, she found he was very kind and a good listener. Alice saw the psychologist for seven months and over that time tried different techniques to stop harming herself. These were progessive muscle relaxation, deep breathing exercises, writing in a diary, playing video games and outdoor exercise. Eventually she found a few techniques that she particularly liked and that worked well for her.

Alice has stopped using self-harm completely and now takes each day as it comes.

Risk factors for developing self-harm

Risk factors for self-harm are similar to those of other mental illnesses and include:

- suffering from a mood or anxiety disorder
- experiencing any sort of trauma while growing up such as bullying, sexual, physical or emotional abuse, the death of a friend or relative
- feeling pressures at school or work
- using street drugs or alcohol
- having family tensions
- knowing friends who engage in deliberate self-harm
- feeling disaffected, disaffiliated and isolated from other people (which makes talking to other people about problems almost impossible).

Some patients have confessed to me that they self-harm because one or more of their friends began to engage in the behaviour and they felt a desire to join in. Once they started doing it, they said it became addictive and the default way to deal with difficult feelings. The harm distracted them from emotional pain (grief or guilt), relieved tension, and indirectly let others around (including parents) know how distressed they were feeling.

Signs and symptoms of self-harm

It can be very difficult to diagnose self-harm because young people who self-mutilate often feel guilty and ashamed about their behaviour, and may try to hide it.

The most common symptoms include:

- cutting wrists, arms, thighs or legs with a sharp object such as razorblade, knife or, most commonly, glass
- carving or burning
- punching or scratching
- piercing with needles
- banging the head
- pressing the eyes
- biting fingers, lips or arms

- pulling hair
- picking at skin.

Rarely, in very extreme cases, self-mutilation can involve broken bones, amputation, castration or suicide.

Diagnosis and treatment of self-harm

Some parents and professionals mistake deliberate self-harm as attention-seeking behaviour that is best ignored. This is unwise for two reasons. Firstly, a 2005 study published in the *American Journal of Psychiatry* found a thirty-fold increase in risk of suicide among self-harmers compared with the general population and secondly, for some young people self-harm can become the default position for coping, despite the potential for permanent physical damage and the destruction of family relationships.

It is important to distinguish between self-harm and suicide attempts. To the untrained observer, unsuccessful suicide attempts can look very much like self-harm, so understanding what lies behind the self-harm is critical.

All young people who self-harm should be professionally assessed. Initial management involves medical treatment for the physical injuries and advice on harm-minimisation techniques (such as how to keep piercing and cutting implements sterile) until the reasons for the self-harming behaviour are identified and brought under control.

As I have said throughout this book, the first port of call for all parents who are worried about their teenager's mental health is the family GP. Under the new Medicare arrangement (as outlined in Chapter 5) GPs should refer them to a specialist mental health worker or an agency such as headspace.

Treatment involves educating the young person, their family members and friends, and psychological counselling (cognitive behavioural therapy, dialectical behaviour therapy as well as acceptance and commitment therapy. In some instances anti-depressant medication will be prescribed (especially where depression is an underlying factor) and the young person taught other more helpful ways of dealing with painful emotions.

MY PARENTS DON'T UNDERSTAND ME
HAVE YOU BEEN SLURRING YOUR WORDS?

Chapter 12
Psychosis

The word psychosis literally means 'abnormal condition of the mind', and is a general psychiatric term for a mental state that involves a loss of contact with reality. A young person with psychosis may see, hear or believe things that other people don't experience, leading to anger, fear and confusion.

Psychosis most often occurs in late adolescence or in early adulthood and affects males and females equally, but men usually develop it at an earlier age. About three out of every 100 Australians will experience a psychotic episode in their lives.

Some adolescents develop psychotic symptoms after being physically, emotionally or sexually abused, others following drug experimentation or severe depression. Depending on the type of psychosis (see below), an episode can be truly horrifying for the young sufferer and equally terrifying for their friends and family, who will also need psycho-education and emotional support.

Chris's story

Chris was about 15 when he began smoking dope, and very quickly developed a strong addiction, smoking every day, all hours of the day. One morning he smoked a few joints. He was supposed to call a friend, and did so, but was suddenly overwhelmed by a sense that she was in danger. Chris didn't know why he was besieged by these thoughts, but knew he had to see her so he arranged to meet her in the city. When he got there, she wasn't anywhere to be seen. He says, 'I just started freaking out. I started seeing dead bodies everywhere. They were, like, in pools of blood . . . just everywhere you look. And everyone is just going about their usual day, walking by as if there's nothing there.'

Chris was having a psychotic episode. 'It was one of the scariest experiences of my life. And, you know, it just got so much for me I actually pulled a knife on someone. I have no idea why. Then the, um, the cops intervened and sent me to hospital.'

Chris received antipsychotic medication, which ameliorated his symptoms. However, after his release from hospital, he went straight back to his bad old habits.

Over the next two years he suffered a series of psychotic events, but it wasn't until he was 18 that something finally gave. 'I just got this sudden rush of pain after having a bong, straight through my head from front to back. And, yeah, it was the most excruciating pain I'd ever felt.' Chris didn't link it to the drugs until it started happening every time he had a bong or a joint. Only then did he quit smoking pot.

Chris has never had another psychotic episode and now works as a mentor to other young people suffering from psychosis at the very hospital he was brought to all those years ago. He generously told his story on national television (see it at www.abc.net.au/catalyst/stories/2402434.htm).

Risk factors for developing psychosis

As with many of the mental health problems described in this book, psychosis is thought to be caused by a mixture of genetic factors (which may increase a young person's predisposition to psychosis) and environmental factors such as extreme trauma, brain tumour, depression and even vitamin deficiency. A brief episode can also be triggered by severe sleep deprivation, a high fever, or substance use (particularly illicit drugs like marijuana).

In 2007, *The Lancet* published the results of a meta-analysis of research on the link between marijuana (cannabis) use and the development of schizophrenia and other mental disorders. The research showed that smoking marijuana at any stage increased your risk of developing a psychotic illness by 40 per cent.

Marijuana use in early adolescence places young people at especially high risk. A 2006 New Zealand study found that adolescents with a certain version of the COMT gene (associated with dopamine production in the brain) who smoked cannabis just once a month were ten times as likely to develop schizophrenia.

Signs and symptoms of psychosis

Psychosis in young people is characterised by a diverse group of symptoms including disorganised thinking, mood problems, personality changes and hallucinations or delusional beliefs. These symptoms may be accompanied by unusual or outlandish behaviour as well as an inability to interact socially, which can prevent normal activities.

In a serious psychotic illness the affected teenager will usually be unaware that there is a problem and will be completely baffled as to why those around them aren't experiencing what they are hearing, smelling, tasting and seeing. The most common symptoms are hearing voices, delusions and feelings of paranoia.

Types of psychosis

Every young person's experience of psychosis is different and doctors are often hesitant to assign a precise label in the early stages. Orygen Youth Health, a Melbourne-based service that assists young people with psychosis, says the illness falls into seven categories.

Drug-induced psychosis

Using or withdrawing from alcohol or drugs can induce psychotic symptoms. Sometimes these symptoms will rapidly disappear as the effects of the drugs/alcohol wear off. In other cases, the illness may last longer.

Brief reactive psychosis

Psychotic symptoms arise suddenly in response to a major stress in the person's life, such as a death in the family, losing a job, diagnosis of a major illness or another dramatic life change. The person makes a quick recovery in only a few days.

Schizophrenia

This is a psychotic illness in which the changes in behaviour or symptoms have been continuing for a period of at least six months. Contrary to media stereotypes, it does not mean the sufferer has a 'split personality'. Many people with schizophrenia lead happy and fulfilling lives, and some make a full recovery.

Bipolar (manic-depressive) disorder

This is where the sufferer experiences extreme changes in mood, alternating between highs (mania) and lows (depression). Psychotic features such as delusions and hallucinations can sometimes manifest during the manic phase, and more rarely during the depressive phase. (See Chapter 3 for more information about bipolar disorder.)

Schizophreniform disorder

This is similar to schizophrenia in that it also distorts the way a person thinks, acts, expresses emotions, perceives reality and relates to others, but the symptoms last for less time, and the sufferer usually recovers in six months. About one person in 1000 develops schizophreniform disorder during his or her lifetime. If the symptoms do not improve, the person is likely to have schizophrenia, which is a life-long illness. According to the American Psychiatric Association, about two-thirds of people with schizophreniform disorder go on to develop schizophrenia.

Schizoaffective disorder

A person with schizoaffective disorder has severe changes in mood as well as some of the psychotic symptoms of schizophrenia, such as hallucinations, delusions and disorganised thinking. Because people with schizoaffective disorder have symptoms of two separate mental illnesses – schizophrenia and a mood disorder – they are often incorrectly diagnosed. As a result, it is difficult to determine the number of sufferers. Estimates suggest that about one in every 200 people (0.5 per cent) develop schizoaffective disorder at some time during his or her life, usually between the ages of 16 and 30.

Diagnosis and treatment of psychosis

While drug-induced or reactive psychosis may well dissipate after a short time, other kinds of psychosis are serious long-term illnesses requiring professional treatment. More often than not, the young person presents to a GP via a third party, sometimes a parent, friend, staff member from school or police officer. This is mostly because psychotic teenagers do not have any understanding of what is happening to them.

When friends or family members try to discuss the teenager's behaviour with them, the young person often refuses to acknowledge a problem or seek help, as they do not see that there is anything wrong with them. They may also respond in a violent or aggressive manner, damaging property or physically harming themselves or others. In such cases a home visit by a Crisis Assessment Team is warranted. (See Chapter 4 for more about CAT teams.)

The standard treatment for a young person with psychosis is antipsychotic medication. There are two types: typical (or traditional) and atypical. The traditional antipsychotic medications were first developed in the 1950s, and have many more side effects than the newer atypicals, which are more commonly prescribed. Atypicals include olanzapine (Zyprexa), amisulpride (Solian), quetiapine (Seroquel), risperidone (Risperdal) and aripiprazole (Abilify). Such medications are frequently helpful in alleviating the symptoms, but are rarely enough by themselves. In an ideal situation, the drug treatment should be accompanied by group therapy, family counselling, psychotherapy and/or cognitive behavioural therapy.

As with all mental illnesses, the earlier the diagnosis and treatment, the better the prognosis. According to Orygen Youth Health, psychotic illnesses are all treatable. In some cases symptoms clear up speedily and young people take up their normal life with little impediment, while others take weeks or months to regain their old level of functioning. Some teenagers will require drug treatment and intensive psychological support throughout their lives. If they refuse treatment and support, the consequences can be catastrophic. In one Swedish study, patients with schizophrenia were followed up for ten years after diagnosis. In that time, 25 per cent had attempted to end their lives, and 2.5 per cent had committed suicide.

As mentioned earlier, adolescents with psychotic illnesses often do not understand what is happening to them or, if they do, harbour fears of being labelled 'insane'. Most will not seek help on their own. Parents, friends and relatives, armed with the right knowledge, are in a good position to help young people get an accurate diagnosis and appropriate treatment. As the world expert on your son or daughter, it is crucial for you to take a lead, become their advocate and seek expert guidance and advice, especially in light of the high levels of mortality associated with this illness. Orygen Youth Health's website (see Resources) provides great fact sheets on psychosis.

WAR
1939–45
PEACE
2003–09
TANDBERG

Chapter 13
Youth suicide

If you ask a group of Australian parents what they want for their children as they become adults, most will say they want them to be happy and healthy. But as we have seen, a teenager's emotional wellbeing can be difficult to assess and in some tragic cases, young people take their own lives before they are out of their teens.

Suicide is devastating for everyone who knew and loved the person – family, friends, school and work colleagues – but often for the wider community as well. There is a particular poignancy when the suicide is that of a young person at the threshold of adulthood.

While the rate of suicide in Australia has actually decreased in recent years, the Australian Bureau of Statistics reports that in 2004–06, suicide still accounted for 20 per cent of the deaths among people aged 15 to 24. And because some suicides are mistaken for accidents (train and car accidents, drug overdoses, drowning), the true figure may well be higher. In May 2008, Suicide Prevention Australia chairman Dr Michael Dudley estimated that suicide figures are under-reported by as much as 13 to 15 per cent.

The highest rates of completed youth suicide tend to be in young males. Girls have higher rates of depression and are actually much more likely to attempt to take their own lives but tend to use less lethal methods and are more likely to ask for help when they feel that they can no longer cope.

While suicidal thoughts are fairly common in adolescence, an Australian study has reported that only 6.6 per cent of adolescents who had thought about suicide had made one or more attempts. Research and clinical practice suggests that it is relatively unusual for young people to think about suicide seriously enough to actually set a date, or develop a plan.

Risk factors for suicide

Suicide is the result of an immensely complex interplay of social, psychological, neurological, biological and cultural variables. The problem is that these variables carry unequal weights and no single one has been demonstrated to be necessary or sufficient to cause an individual to take their own life. This makes it very difficult to predict whether a young person is likely to commit suicide, and therefore difficult for others to act in time to prevent it.

Many young people have times when they think about killing or harming themselves, usually because the distress they are feeling is too much for them to cope with and they feel an overwhelming loss of hope. This distress can be caused by many things including the death of somebody close, fights with parents and/or friends, relationship break-ups, problems at school, bullying and sexual or emotional abuse.

A series of psychological autopsy studies over the last few decades has identified several of the most important risk factors.

Pre-existing mental illness

Studies show that 90 per cent of young people who end their lives have a mental disorder at the time of their death, the most common being depression, psychosis, substance abuse disorders, eating disorders and personality disorders. Recent studies suggest that if these mental disorders co-occur – for example if a young person has depression and a substance abuse disorder – the risk of suicide is substantially elevated.

Previous suicide attempts

Another significant risk factor is whether a young person has made a previous suicide attempt. In a longitudinal study of suicide in Christchurch, New Zealand (the Canterbury Suicide Project), it was found that of 129 people who had made a medically serious attempt on their lives, 53.3 per cent had made previous attempts.

Socioeconomic disadvantage

Another risk factor is social disadvantage, for example, coming from a family with a low annual income and having parents with poor or no educational qualifications and high rates of residential mobility.

Subtle signs of suicidal behaviour

A substantial proportion of young people who are suicidal give subtle warnings that they are intending to take their own lives. These warnings may be direct or indirect, but in many cases are commented on in retrospect by people who were close to them. Direct statements from young people thinking of ending their own lives include the following:

- 'You would be better off without me.'
- 'I wish I was dead.'
- 'I just want to go to sleep and never wake up again.'
- 'Life is not worth living.'
- 'I wish I could disappear forever.'

Adolescents intending to kill themselves often ask questions about death or heaven, write songs or poetry about death, or read books about death and dying. Morbid themes may dominate their artwork or music, and they may become obsessed with TV programs about murder or death and weapons.

Another sign may be sudden calmness after an intense period of depression, anxiety or other mental illness. Once they have made the decision to end their life, some feel such relief at the thought of being able to escape their unmanageable feelings that their mood improves noticeably. It is important, therefore, to be alert to signs of depression, either on its own or as part of another mental illness. Signs to look for include:

- drug or alcohol abuse
- loss of interest in things they used to enjoy
- withdrawal, irritability or more marked personality changes
- violent behaviour
- running away from home, truancy
- change in eating and/or sleeping habits
- poor concentration
- lack of care with appearance, schoolwork etc.

Lucy's story

Dear Mum

I know that, after what I've done, probably the last thing you want to be doing right now is reading some shit letter full of 'sorrys', excuses and 'I love yous' but I felt I needed to write something – for closure I suppose, and to make sure that something nice isn't left unsaid forever.

And yes. I do realise the full extent of this decision, and its consequences. I know (I hate it, but I know it) that I will be hurting people by doing this, you are probably at the top of the list, and it tears me apart to think that I am causing people I love that amount of intense pain, but as I have said – it has just got to a point where this hell outweighs EVERYTHING – yes, even the strongest thing in my life – love. But I am not here to make excuses. I realise that death is permanent. It is forever. It is the end. Final. That is, I suppose, why it seems so attractive to me – my brain and body will never have this overload of intense emotion and agony. Yeah, I wonder about some afterlife, maybe it will happen. Is there a small chance I will remember this life? All unknown to me, occasionally scary, but whatever it is, whether it be nothing or something, it is different.

So, now I am physically dead, mentally gone. I don't appear to be anything anymore, other than a corpse (ps – I want to be cremated and sprinkled either at Torquay, or at school). But am I really gone? You can't hug me, but maybe you can still feel me. You can't converse with me but we are still connected. You can't do things with me, but there are memories, I hope they are good ones, really good ones. I know I will always be there, in some part of you, or near you, and let's face it, we all have to go sometime, just for me, I died of depression, rather than cancer, heart disease, or a car accident. Suicide is not what killed me, it is this lingering depression that killed me long ago. I have just now taken a small, final step in the death it is causing, by physically ending my life.

I know that nothing I can say will make this shit that I put you in any more bearable, nor will I be able to shed some light on this awful situation, but the most important thing for me now is to let you know how much I love you. On paper, after my death, I can't imagine it meaning a lot, other than three short words, but I love you more than you know, more than you can even imagine or comprehend. They say that the strongest love connection is the one that a mother has for her daughter. Not having given birth myself, I have no idea, but I loved you like a child. I worried about you, I wanted to protect you, to be there for you and help you. I loved you as a friend, as a mother, as a support and as someone that I could not live without. I hope (but fear this is not the case) that you can live without me. I am just one person, one body, one soul. There are so many others that care for you and for whom you care and love. Part of you (me) is gone, but I hope that you can fill the emptiness, or at least make it seem less empty, with those around you, and with things you love. You have so many wonderful people who love and care for you, and that will support you.

Quote: 'Suicide is not a choice. It is simply a state that occurs when pain outweighs coping'. My pain outweighed my coping long ago. It was you that gave me these extra months (probably more like years), on my life. This is not a personal attack on you or anyone else, and I have thought about the consequences that may arise from it. I have properly thought this through. I'm just sorry it had to be this way.

Please don't forget how much I love you, and please tell Dad, Kate and my friends the messages in this letter, and most important – don't feel guilty! It's not your fault! I convinced them at The Inpatient unit I would be safe, as I did you. I killed myself. You didn't, you couldn't have stopped me.

Uh, I can't even express how much I love you. Soooooo much.

Please forgive me.

Love from

Lucy

This letter was written by a 17-year-old Australian girl ('Lucy' is not her real name) moments before she ended her life.

Lucy's mother remembers her daughter being an unusually contented and happy baby. Later, while other toddlers were beginning to pull each other's hair, and bite and scratch, Lucy sat in the corner happily eating a carrot stick and playing with an educational toy of some sort.

As a child, she adored jigsaws and puzzles, and every birthday she received more challenging toys and strategic games. She was also a voracious reader and a frequent visitor to the local library.

At kindergarten, Lucy proved to be very attentive and studious. She worked very hard to impress the teacher, but somehow managed to get through three-year-old kinder and halfway through four-year-old kinder without letting on that she could read and do maths problems. In fact, the teacher discovered her abilities quite by accident, and approached her mother excitedly to tell her what she already knew. Her mum had suspected that Lucy was quite advanced, but didn't want to be the over-zealous parent. Also, as Lucy was her first child, she wasn't sure just how advanced she was. The kinder teacher was beside herself, and suggested to the family that Lucy be tested for 'giftedness' at a specialist centre at a local university. The tests indicated that she was indeed well advanced for her age, but her parents confessed to having no idea how to raise a 'gifted' child.

Her mother wrote to me:

I've said it for a long time now, that it is much the same as having a child with a learning disability. If your child has an intelligence level in the bottom 3% of the population, they qualify for assistance with their own teacher's aide and special curriculum to assist them through their school years. If your child sits in the top 3%, as Lucy did, there is nothing at all available for them. These kids need extra help, just in different ways. We were so fortunate that Lucy was studious, so she worked quietly and diligently, finishing her work quickly then waiting for the next task. Unfortunately, this meant that she spent a huge proportion of her school life waiting for something else to do. I spoke to every teacher and principal along the way, encouraging them to be creative and think of ways to stimulate this kid, but very few listened. At year six level, the teacher brought in a secondary maths teacher to provide extra work to keep Lucy stimulated, but she ripped through this and was still left waiting for more to do. My pathetic attempt to help her overcome this unendurable waiting was to say that eventually she would go to university and meet like-minded people and be stimulated with new and exciting knowledge at every turn. I think she grasped onto this thought for many years, but it didn't really help resolve the problems at school.

In year five, we had Lucy sit the scholarship tests for local private schools. We were astounded when she was offered a 100% scholarship to Ballarat Grammar from Year 6 to Year 12! The school proved to be a very supportive environment, not only for Lucy as her depression increased, but for her sister Kate [who was born when Lucy was two and a half] and our family over the worst times.

When Lucy was in Year 6 her mother decided to stop studying law because she felt Lucy needed extra attention. At this point, things started to go awry. Lucy discovered that she needed to wear spectacles, which she hated, and she still hadn't found a social group she fitted into. Her family maintain she was bullied by the boys, who called her a nerd, but she was also more subtly excluded by the 'popular' girls.

Music featured very prominently in her life from this time. Previously, she had enjoyed playing recorder and clarinet, but she always aspired to play the saxophone. Once she got her hands on one, she loved it as she thought she would. She worked very quickly through the Australian Music Examinations Board grades, to complete the highest level within four and a half years. She kept herself further stimulated by having lessons in cello and piano at various times. She could read music like others read books, so it was quite easy for her to play any instrument. But when she gradually stopped playing, it was a clear sign that things were not right with her.

In October 2006, when Lucy was in Year 10, her mother received a phone call at work informing her that her daughter had taken an overdose and that the school was arranging to have her taken to hospital. This was like being hit by a truck. The family knew she hadn't been herself, but didn't realise the extent of her unhappiness.

After Lucy was discharged from the emergency department, the family went to the local child and adolescent mental health service for a session. She was given her treatment options, and she chose to pursue no treatment. This was considered a valid choice by the staff because she was considered a competent minor. Her mother asked how she could be deemed competent when she had just tried to kill herself, but this was never satisfactorily answered.

Her mother did not agree with this outcome, and found a very sympathetic and kind GP who managed, over several weeks, to convince Lucy to commence treatment. She started on some antidepressants which, after another attempted overdose, appeared to help for a while. Lucy still had not told her friends and had forbidden her parents to tell her extended family about her illness.

Over the next months the medication failed her, and the GP considered she was a very high suicide risk. She referred Lucy to a psychiatrist in Melbourne, who recommended Lucy be admitted to the Royal Children's Hospital's inpatient unit. This is a specialist unit designed to look after acutely mentally ill young people and stabilise them – in other words to get them to a stage where they are no longer a danger to themselves.

Over the next three months she tried two more antidepressants with no success. Another more serious overdose followed (she had done further research this time and her methods were becoming more efficient), and Lucy talked to her mother about her complete despair, her belief that nothing would help her and that she would never get better. In moments of major crisis when she was not in hospital, usually on the weekends, there was nothing the family could do to get support. The advice was always to call the police and/or ambulance. As her mother wrote to me:

No-one wants to call the police on their own child, so we would just manage as best as we could. We felt as though we were being let down but we didn't really know who to turn to.

Her last admission to the inpatient unit lasted five weeks. She was at such high risk that the family were only able to take her on three short outings in that time. On two of those three occasions she tried to abscond.

What happened next still causes the family bewilderment. As her mother wrote:

I received a phone call saying that Lucy would be coming home on weekend leave. I questioned this, given that she was continuing to worsen and was still clearly expressing her desire to kill herself. They stated that Lucy had given them assurances, and that they believed she was not at risk at that time. Two days later, Lucy phoned her sister to say that she intended to commit suicide on the weekend, and that she wanted to say goodbye. Despite this, the hospital said the visit could go ahead.

Her mother collected her on the Friday night from the unit. Her sister chose to stay at a friend's house that night. (Lucy's mother was well aware that it would be too much of a burden for her other daughter to be expected to help supervise or support her older sister.) Lucy seemed to be okay, chatting with her mother as they drove home. She tried to say goodbye, but her mother dismissed this and told her she couldn't do it because it would hurt too many people. They went to bed separately (her mum had offered to share her bed but Lucy had declined) and when her mum woke in the morning, she was relieved to find that she was still alive. Because nights were always hardest, Lucy's mother felt she could leave Lucy alone for half an hour while she walked the dogs. Afterwards, they had planned to go shopping and somewhere nice for lunch.

When her mother returned from the walk, she found her daughter hanging from the back porch. She was white and cold and her mother knew she had been there from the moment she had left the house. Her mother cut her down and began resuscitation. Lucy's heart started after the longest time, and she ended up in intensive care. She remained there, in a persistent vegetative state, for almost three weeks after which she was allowed to die peacefully at the family's request.

This was one of many instances where the family and mental health professionals did *everything* in their power to help a young person overcome a mental illness. Sometimes, however, a person's brain chemistry can become so unbalanced that no amount of love and caring or trying to build up confidence, optimism or self-esteem can alter their sense of futility and hopelessness.

Suicide prevention

Picking up on the sometimes subtle signs of depression in your teenager and *taking action* are major factors in suicide prevention. (See Chapter 3 for more on depression, and Chapter 4 for advice on seeking treatment.) Without a sensitively conducted, adolescent-friendly assessment by a knowledgeable professional who can help establish rapport, assess risk, diagnose the nature and extent of the problem and develop a treatment plan one can never be entirely sure that the young person is completely safe.

Research has shown that only one in five young people aged 16 to 24 with suicidal thoughts would be willing to ask for help from their doctor – they just need help from their parents to get them there in the first place.

If young people are diagnosed as actively suicidal, ideally they should be hospitalised, but sometimes this is not possible and they may be sent home and parents told to 'take precautions' or go on 'suicide watch'. This means that parents should ensure that all firearms, cutting instruments, alcohol and medications are securely locked away. They need to be extra vigilant, and must never ask peers or siblings to supervise, as this places too great a burden on other young people and could create a major trauma if they were unable to prevent a successful suicide attempt.

Parents who create an encouraging, supportive, stable home environment with adequate supervision can substantially decrease the young person's feelings of distress. However, you can only act on what you know at the time. Knowledge is power, so in such situations try to get as much information as possible. Never be afraid to seek a second opinion if you are unsure about the advice that you receive.

DAD, MUM AND THE TEENAGER

Conclusion

I have written this book so parents not only understand the warning signs of depression and other mental illnesses in young people, but also know how to get the right type of help. The role of parents is critical, as depressed young people usually are not capable of helping themselves – their information processing is often biased, leading to unrealistic and profoundly pessimistic thinking that leaves them convinced nothing will help them.

Sadly, there are some mental health professionals who choose to treat depressed people with medication alone and make no attempt to explore the causes of their illness, or give them the tools to manage relapses. More than 75 per cent of depressive illness is directly triggered by stressful life events, and research shows that cognitive behavioural therapy is just as effective as medication at relieving distress.

While beyondblue and other organisations such as SANE,

youth beyondblue, Reach Out, headspace, Lifeline, Kids Helpline, MoodGYM, MindMatters and Orygen Youth Health are doing a brilliant job raising awareness of mental illness, headspace is the only real on-the-ground organisation with clinical support. It's a start, but opening hours are still inadequate and funding an ongoing issue.

Australia needs more of these youth-appropriate services, but we also need to make better use of technology. The internet (and also mobile phones) offers great possibilities to empower young people to plan their wellbeing and *prevent* illness (rather than use online sources to manage disease). Young people spend increasing amounts of time online, and with the latest innovations in web design technology, it will be possible to create online 'wellbeing' centres or 'virtual clinics' that share information, maintain health records, facilitate mood mapping and are linked to community centres such as headspace.

Whatever happens, we need to do something. Professor Pat McGorry, head of the Orygen Research Centre and one of Australia's leading experts on youth mental health, told *The Age* newspaper last year that the prevalence of mental health problems had not declined in ten years, suggesting a systemic failure in treatment. He argued that the federal government had failed to realise how much investment and political support was needed to address the problem.

Aside from prevention, I think one of the biggest issues is early diagnosis and treatment. We need funding advocacy at a high enough level to keep experienced clinicians in public health so that young people can be assessed and treated quickly by an appropriate psychiatrist. Sadly, there seems to be a paucity of appropriately trained adolescent psychiatrists, and in fact they are amongst the poorest distributed of all medical specialists.

Instead many families find themselves stuck in the system, following the correct procedures to try to find the best professional who can 'connect' with their teenager. This takes a lot of time – time that sometimes the Hannahs and Lucys of this world just don't have.

The establishment of rapport with a young person is critical. Someone like Hannah Modra would not have just opened up – she would have needed to get to know someone before she trusted them with the awful truth of her illness, which she regarded as a weakness. The fact is that disengagement is common. This is where the young person gives up trying to get help because they feel the professional does not understand them and has nothing to offer them. The young person feels they are just wasting the professional's time.

Parents, too, can become frustrated, especially with the issue of confidentiality. Psychologists, psychiatrists and general practitioners are required by law to stick to the 'mature minor' doctrine, which allows teenagers to give consent to treatment as long as the practitioner thinks that the young person shows sufficient maturity and understanding of what is going on and can appreciate the consequences of the proposed treatment or procedures on offer.

What would make a difference is a 'mentor' model, where someone is assigned to a young person to help them negotiate the system and actually sticks with them for the whole journey, rather than the young person accumulating a series of case managers who only keep a file. This is particularly useful when treatment involves multiple professionals (GP, psychologist, psychiatrist, paediatrician) and agencies.

Experience shows that schools that have practices and policies about discussing depression openly and teach young people help-seeking behaviours do make a difference.

Does your teenager's school:

- use the Mind Matters curriculum material that has been endorsed by successive federal governments?
- introduce students to free computer programs such as www.moodgym.anu.edu.au or free computer games that teach their kids life skills such as www.reachoutcentral.com.au?
- request that its teachers are signed up to the teacher's mental health website www.reachoutpro.com.au?
- have the Kids Helpline logo and number (1800 551 800) as the standard screen saver on all the school's computers?
- advertise the free online counselling service that Kids Helpline offers?
- invite local GPs in each year to teach young people how to

access their own Medicare card and explain the process of getting help and their rights to confidentiality?

Of course, even if every school in Australia ticks these boxes, the sad fact remains that families will continue to bury their children who have died by their own hand, and sit by the grave in an agony of grief and unanswered questions.

The last thing Hannah did before ending her life was to log on to the beyondblue website – but she clearly did not find what she was looking for in time. The truth is that Hannah's illness was so far advanced that there was probably nothing that could have been put on any website that could have prevented the terrible events that followed. Because sometimes depression descends so quickly and/or is so severe that only a miracle can save those affected. Hannah and Lucy had no miracle, but if their stories can act as a catalyst to prevent the death of just one other, then their telling has been worthwhile.

Resources

American Academy of Child and Adolescent psychiatry
www.aacap.org
The American Academy of Child and Adolescent Psychiatry site aims to assist parents and families to understand a wide range of emotional and mental disorders affecting children and young people. It includes a glossary of terms frequently used, American statistics and the latest information on children and psychiatric medication.

Auseinet
www.auseinet.com
This is the site of the Australian Network for Promotion, Prevention and Early Intervention for Mental Health, which aims to assist a range of sectors to implement mental health promotion and illness prevention approaches in their respective settings. These settings include, but are not limited to, mental health and

health services, community organisations, schools, NGOs, educational institutions (such as TAFE and universities), and general practices.

Australian Drug Foundation
www.adf.org.au
A not-for-profit organisation providing information and a range of services and programs designed to prevent alcohol and other drug problems.

Australian Psychological Society
www.psychology.org.au
1 800 333 497
A psychologist can help by diagnosing and treating problems such as anxiety, depression or eating disorders and equipping young people and their families with the skills needed to function better. This site offers a referral service to members of the Australian Psychological Society in private practice who deal with particular problems.

Beyondblue

www.beyondblue.org.au

This site provides information on depression and anxiety, including available treatments and where to find help. The mission of beyondblue is to increase the capacity of the broader Australian community to prevent depression and respond effectively. This website includes some simple checklists that are quick, easy and anonymous.

Black Dog Institute

www.blackdoginstitute.org.au

The Black dog Institute is the brainchild of the inspirational Professor Gordon Parker, who put together an informative website specialising in mood disorders. It has loads of expert advice on depression and bipolar disorder along with advice on how to get help and stay well.

BlueBoard

www.blueboard.anu.edu.au

This is an online support group for people affected by depression, bipolar disorder and anxiety disorders. It aims to reduce stigma, and to provide support, hope and opportunities for sharing successful coping strategies. The group is run as a moderated bulletin board with strict protocols to enhance safety and privacy.

BluePages

www.bluepages.anu.edu.au

This site provides information about depression and its treatment. It includes reviews of the available scientific evidence for a wide range of treatments. It also incorporates information about the experience and symptoms of depression and state-based resources for help. Research indicates that use of this site can decrease depressive symptoms.

Bullying

www.bullying.org

This site was developed by Canadian educator Bill Bell, who coined the term cyber bullying, and it provides information, education and training resources with the aim of eliminating bullying.

CanTeen

www.canteen.org.au

CanTeen is a national support organisation for young people living with cancer or who have parents or primary carers with cancer.

Child Support Agency

www.csa.gov.au

This site provides access to the latest forms, publications, brochures, leaflets and other information on child support issues, in an immediate, user-friendly way.

Clinical Research Unit for Anxiety and Depression
www.crufad.org.au
This site provides information about depression and includes a self-help depression quiz, information and advice.

Commonwealth Department of Families, Housing, Community Services and Indigenous Affairs (FaHCSIA)
www.facs.gov.au
1800 260 402
The department provides policies, support and assistance retraining families and communities and individuals.

Drug Info
www.druginfo.adf.org.au
DrugInfo Clearinghouse is a program of the Australian Drug Foundation. This site provides easy access to information about alcohol and other drugs, and drug abuse prevention.

DirectLine
1800 888 236

If you live in the state of Victoria and someone you care about has an alcohol or drug problem, you can call DirectLine to talk to professional counsellors who are experienced in alcohol and drug-related matters. The service is free, anonymous and confidential and provides 24–7 counselling, information and referral.

e-couch
www.ecouch.anu.edu.au

E-hub's newest self-help interactive program includes modules for social anxiety and generalised anxiety as well as depression. It provides self-help interventions drawn from cognitive, behavioural and interpersonal therapies as well as relaxation and physical activity. Modules for panic disorder, bereavement and relationship breakdown are currently being developed.

Early Psychosis Prevention and Intervention Centre
www.eppic.org.au
The Early Psychosis Prevention and Intervention Centre is a comprehensive service directed to young people aged 15 to 30 who are experiencing or who have experienced their first episode of psychosis. There are great fact sheets to help people learn more about the different types of psychosis-spectrum disorders, phases of assessment, treatment and recovery.

Families Matter
www.familiesmatter.org.au
Families Matter has been developed as a necessary complement to MindMatters and seeks to engage parents, carers and families in the health and wellbeing of their young people.

Family Court of Australia
www.familycourt.gov.au
Great information about the Family Court, including tips, forms, do-it-yourself kits and information.

Fatherhood Foundation

www.fathersonline.org

A charitable, not-for-profit organisation with a goal to inspire, encourage and educate men to a greater level of excellence as fathers.

Good Therapy

www.goodtherapy.com.au

Good Therapy Australia is a registered health promotion charity. Its website outlines the various approaches in counselling and psychotherapy and has a directory of practitioners, public-forum articles and an online bookshop.

Headroom

www.headroom.net.au

Headroom is a South Australian website dedicated to the positive mental health of children and adolescents and the adults in their lives.

headspace

www.headspace.org.au

Australia's national youth mental health foundation was established to respond more effectively to young people with mental health, alcohol and substance-abuse problems.

Healthinsite

www.healthinsite.gov.au

This offers a wide range of up-to-date information on health topics such as diabetes, cancer, mental health and asthma.

Kids Helpline

www.kidshelp.com.au

1800 551 800

Kids Helpline (free call from a land line) is Australia's only free, confidential and anonymous telephone and online counselling service specifically for young people aged 5 to 25.

Lawstuff

www.lawstuff.org.au

This website provides information about the legal rights of people under the age of 18. It is sponsored by the National Children and Youth Law Centre – an independent not-for-profit organisation.

Lifeline

www.lifeline.org.au

13 11 14

Longstanding 24–7 telephone counselling service that also provides information and referrals to people with mental health difficulties (and their carers).

Mandometer Clinic

www.mandometer.com.au

The Mandometer Clinic offers treatment for eating disorders using the Mandometer Method. This site explains the technique and can refer to Australian clinics.

Mental Illness Fellowship of Australia

www.mifellowshipaustralia.org.au

The Mental Illness Fellowship of Australia represents people affected by severe mental illness and provides fact sheets to help families and people affected by mental illness.

MindMatters

www.mindmatters.edu.au

The MindMatters program supports Australian secondary schools in promoting and protecting the members of school communities with mental health problems. Each state and territory has a dedicated web page.

MoodGYM

www.moodgym.anu.edu.au

This is a free online CBT program designed to prevent depression and anxiety in young adults. First launched in 2001, this is its third revision.

Multicultural Mental Health Australia

www.mmha.org.au

Information about the mental health and wellbeing of Australians from culturally and linguistically diverse backgrounds including fact sheets in languages other than English.

NetSafe

www.netsafe.org.nz

This is the website of the Internet Safety Group of New Zealand and offers cyber safety education to children, parents, schools, community organisations and businesses. The ISG has been designated the New Zealand Ministry of Education's agent of choice for cyber safety education in New Zealand.

Orygen Youth Health

www.oyh.org.au

Orygen Youth Health (OYH) is Australia's largest youth-focused mental health organisation. It offers a specialised youth mental health clinical service and is an internationally renowned youth mental health research centre. The website has brilliant fact sheets and a series of short web films that raise awareness of mental health issues facing many young people. They are an ideal way to engage and begin discussion in either a classroom or case management setting.

Panic and Anxiety Disorders Assistance
www.pada.org.au
This site provides information and resources for people suffering from anxiety disorders or depression with a view to helping them regain control of their lives. It also offers tips for carers and links to other organisations in the same field.

Parentline
www.parentline.com.au
Parentline is a confidential telephone counselling service aimed at providing professional counselling and support for parents and others who care for children.

PFLAG

www.pflag.org.au

Based in Victoria and Queensland, Parents and Friends of Lesbians and Gays is a support, information and advocacy group.

Reach Out

www.reachout.com.au

A web based program designed to inspire young people to help themselves through tough times. It provides support information and referrals in an appealing and youth-friendly manner.

Reach Out Central

www.reachoutcentral.com.au

This is an amazing downloadable computer game that teaches young people social and emotional competencies such as anger management, problem solving, decision-making and conflict resolution skills.

Royal Australian and New Zealand College of Psychiatrists
www.ranzcp.org/resources/clinical-practice-guidelines.html
This site contains psychiatric clinical guidelines and a series of treatment guides for consumers and carers on the following topics: anorexia nervosa, bipolar disorder, deliberate self-harm, depression, panic disorder, agoraphobia and schizophrenia.

SANE Australia
www.sane.org
SANE Australia is a national charity working for a better life for people affected by mental illness. Fact sheets on mental illness are available.

School Focused Youth Service
www.sfys.infoxchange.net.au
School Focused Youth Service is a federal government initiative designed to augment support provided to schools in response to the recommendations of the suicide prevention taskforce.

Stepfamily

www.stepfamily.asn.au

This website aims to actively promote the positive aspects of step-family life, especially by providing appropriate information.

Triple P – Positive Parenting Program

www.triplep.net

The Positive Parenting Program aims to prevent severe behavioural, emotional and developmental problems in children by enhancing the knowledge, skills and confidence of parents.

youth beyondblue

www.youthbeyondblue.com

Information on depression, anxiety and related substance-use disorders. This site is aimed at young people and provides information, tips, personal stories and links.

Selected references

Barns, G., 'Anxiety can sneak up and drain your spirit during troubled times', *Sydney Morning Herald*, 6 November 2008.

Barry, E., 'Fiona Stanley says 1 in 5 unfit to be parents', *The Sunday Telegraph*, 28 September 2008.

Beautrais, A., Canterbury Suicide Project, University of Otago, at www.chmeds.ac.nz/research/suicide/pdfs/youth_suicide_and_teen_suicide.pdf.

Booth, M., et al., 'Access to health care among NSW adolescents', NSW Centre for the Advancement of Adolescent Health, Children's Hospital at Westmead, New South Wales, 2002, at www.caah.chw.edu.au/resources/access_phase_1_report_final.pdf.

Bulik, C.M., et al., 'Anorexia nervosa treatment: a systematic review of randomized controlled trials', *International Journal of Eating Disorders*, vol. 40, no. 4, May 2007, pp. 310–20.

Court, J., et al., 'An innovative treatment programme for

anorexia nervosa', *Journal of Paediatrics and Child Health*, vol. 41, no. 5–6, May 2005, pp. 1–2.

Cooper, J., et al., 'Suicide After Deliberate Self-Harm: A 4-Year Cohort Study', *American Journal of Psychiatry*, vol. 162, no. 2, February 2005, pp. 297–303.

De Leo, D. & Heller, T.S., 'Who are the kids who self-harm? An Australian self-report school survey', *Medical Journal of Australia*, vol. 181, no. 3, 2 August 2004, pp. 140–44 at mja.com.au/public/issues/181_03_020804/del10634_fm.pdf.

Dulcan, M., 'Practice Parameters for the assessment and treatment of children, adolescents, and adults with attention-deficit/hyperactivity disorder', *Journal of the American Academy of Child and Adolescent Psychiatry*, vol. 36, no. 10, October 1997, pp. 85S–121S.

'First drug approved for seasonal depression', John Hopkins Depression and Anxiety Bulletin, January 2007, at johnshopkinshealthalerts.com/alerts/depression_anxiety/JohnsHopkinsDepressionAnxietyHealthAlert_695-1.html.

Goldenring, J. & Cohen, E., 'HEADSS – the psycho-social

review of systems with teenagers', *Contemporary Pediatrics*, vol. 5, July 1988, pp. 90–5.

Golding J., et al., 'ALSPAC – the Avon Longitudinal Study of Parents and Children', *Paediatric & Perinatal Epidemiology,* vol. 15, no. 1, *January* 2001, pp. 74–87.

Logan, A. C., 'Omega-3 fatty acids and major depression: a primer for the mental health professional', *Lipids in Health and Disease*, vol. 3, no. 25, November 2004.

'Illicit Drug Use Starts with Cannabis', The Dunedin *Multidisciplinary Health* and *Development Study*, University of Otago, 14 March 2006, at otago.ac.nz/news/news/2006/14-03-06_press_release.html.

'Mental health', Australian Bureau of Statistics, 2009, at http://www.ausstats.abs.gov.au/ausstats/subscriber.nsf/LookupAttach/4102.0Publication25.03.094/$File/41020_Mentalhealth.pdf.

Metlikovec, J. & Walliker, A., 'Teenager suicides at shock rate', *Herald Sun*, 31 May 2008.

Moore, T., 'Cannabis use and risk of psychotic or affective

mental health outcomes: a systematic review', *The Lancet*, vol. 370, no. 9584, 28 July 2007, pp. 319–28.

'Report of the APA Task Force on the Sexualization of Girls', American Psychological Association, 2007, at www.apa.org/pi/wpo/sexualizationsum.html.

'Risk taking by young people', Australian Bureau of Statistics, 2008, at abs.gov.au/AUSSTATS/abs@.nsf/Lookup/4102.0Chapter5002008.

Stark, J., 'Mental illness ravaging nation's youth', *The Age*, 24 October 2008.

Sagduyu, K. et al., 'Omega-3 fatty acids decreased irritability of patients with bipolar disorder', *Nutrition Journal*, vol. 4, no. 6, February 2005.

'Schizophreniform Disorder', Schizophrenia Guide, at webmd.com/schizophrenia/guide/mental-health-schizophreniform-disorder

Schweitzer, R., et al., 'Suicide ideation and behaviours among university students in Australia', *Australian and New Zealand Journal of Psychiatry*, vol. 29, no. 3, September 1995, pp. 473–9.

Tucci, J., et al., 'The Concerns of Australian Parents', Australian Childhood Foundation, 2004.

Veit, F., et al., 'Barriers to effective primary health care for adolescents', *Medical Journal of Australia*, vol. 165, no. 3, 5 August 1996, pp. 131–3.

Vieth, R., et al., 'Randomized comparison of the effects of the vitamin D3 adequate intake versus 100 mcg per day on biochemical responses and the wellbeing of patients', *Nutrition Journal*, vol. 3, no. 8, July 2004.

Wallace, N., 'Doctors don't dish out Ritalin: report', *Sydney Morning Herald*, 12 February 2008, p. 5.

'Young Australians: their health and wellbeing', Australian Institute of Health and Welfare, 2007, at aihw.gov.au/publications/index.cfm/title/10451.

Further reading

Burns, David D., *The Feeling Good Handbook,* Penguin, New York, 1999.

Phillips, Katharine, *The Broken Mirror: Understanding and Treating Body Dysmorphic Disorder*, Oxford University Press, Oxford, 1996.

Swets, Paul, *The Art of Talking with Your Teenager*, Adams Media Corp, Holbrook, 1995.

Wever, Chris, *The Secret Problem*, 3rd ed., Shrink-Rap Press, Australia, 2006.

Wilhelm, Sabine, *Feeling Good about the Way You Look: A Program for Overcoming Body Image Problems,* The Guilford Press, New York, 2006.

Acknowledgements

This book would not have been possible without the assistance of some truly wonderful and inspiring people. First, the families and young people who have generously allowed me to share their stories in order that others might be helped.

Second, Jason Clarke and Dr Simon Kinsella for their unstinting help and support in reviewing the manuscript.

Third, to my family who have once again brought me endless cups of tea and offered love and encouragement throughout the writing process.

Lastly to the wonderfully calm, efficient and encouraging Miriam Cannell, who has earnt a place in the pantheon of wonderful editors, to the genius that is Ron Tandberg and to publisher Ali Watts who has been there for all four Penguin books. Roll on, number five!

Index